IT HAPPENED TO ME

Series Editor: Arlene Hirschfelder

Books in the It Happened to Me series are designed for inquisitive teens digging for answers about certain illnesses, social issues, or lifestyle interests. Whether you are deep into your teen years or just entering them, these books are gold mines of up-to-date information, riveting teen views, and great visuals to help you figure out stuff. Besides special boxes highlighting singular facts, each book is enhanced with the latest reading lists, websites, and an index. Perfect for browsing, there are loads of expert information by acclaimed writers to help parents, guardians, and librarians understand teen illness, tough situations, and lifestyle choices.

1. *Epilepsy: The Ultimate Teen Guide,* by Kathlyn Gay and Sean McGarrahan, 2002.
2. *Stress Relief: The Ultimate Teen Guide,* by Mark Powell, 2002.
3. *Learning Disabilities: The Ultimate Teen Guide,* by Penny Hutchins Paquette and Cheryl Gerson Tuttle, 2003.
4. *Making Sexual Decisions: The Ultimate Teen Guide,* by L. Kris Gowen, 2003.
5. *Asthma: The Ultimate Teen Guide,* by Penny Hutchins Paquette, 2003.
6. *Cultural Diversity—Conflicts and Challenges: The Ultimate Teen Guide,* by Kathlyn Gay, 2003.
7. *Diabetes: The Ultimate Teen Guide,* by Katherine J. Moran, 2004.
8. *When Will I Stop Hurting? Teens, Loss, and Grief: The Ultimate Teen Guide to Dealing with Grief,* by Ed Myers, 2004.
9. *Volunteering: The Ultimate Teen Guide,* by Kathlyn Gay, 2004.
10. *Organ Transplants—A Survival Guide for the Entire Family: The Ultimate Teen Guide,* by Tina P. Schwartz, 2005.
11. *Medications: The Ultimate Teen Guide,* by Cheryl Gerson Tuttle, 2005.
12. *Image and Identity—Becoming the Person You Are: The Ultimate Teen Guide,* by L. Kris Gowen and Molly C. McKenna, 2005.
13. *Apprenticeship: The Ultimate Teen Guide,* by Penny Hutchins Paquette, 2005.
14. *Cystic Fibrosis: The Ultimate Teen Guide,* by Melanie Ann Apel, 2006.
15. *Religion and Spirituality in America: The Ultimate Teen Guide,* by Kathlyn Gay, 2006.
16. *Gender Identity: The Ultimate Teen Guide,* by Cynthia L. Winfield, 2007.

17. *Physical Disabilities: The Ultimate Teen Guide,* by Denise Thornton, 2007.

18. *Money—Getting It, Using It, and Avoiding the Traps: The Ultimate Teen Guide,* by Robin F. Brancato, 2007.

19. *Self-Advocacy: The Ultimate Teen Guide,* by Cheryl Gerson Tuttle and JoAnn Augeri Silva, 2007.

20. *Adopted: The Ultimate Teen Guide,* by Suzanne Buckingham Slade, 2007.

21. *The Military and Teens: The Ultimate Teen Guide,* by Kathlyn Gay, 2008.

22. *Animals and Teens: The Ultimate Teen Guide,* by Gail Green, 2009.

23. *Reaching Your Goals: The Ultimate Teen Guide,* by Anne Courtright, 2009.

24. *Juvenile Arthritis: The Ultimate Teen Guide,* by Kelly Rouba, 2009.

25. *Obsessive-Compulsive Disorder: The Ultimate Teen Guide,* by Natalie Rompella, 2009.

26. *Body Image and Appearance: The Ultimate Teen Guide,* by Kathlyn Gay, 2009.

27. *Writing and Publishing: The Ultimate Teen Guide,* by Tina P. Schwartz, 2010.

28. *Food Choices: The Ultimate Teen Guide,* by Robin F. Brancato, 2010.

29. *Immigration: The Ultimate Teen Guide,* by Tatyana Kleyn, 2011.

30. *Living with Cancer: The Ultimate Teen Guide,* by Denise Thornton, 2011.

31. *Living Green: The Ultimate Teen Guide,* by Kathlyn Gay, 2012.

32. *Social Networking: The Ultimate Teen Guide,* by Jenna Obee, 2012.

33. *Sports: The Ultimate Teen Guide,* by Gail Fay, 2013.

34. *Adopted: The Ultimate Teen Guide, Revised Edition,* by Suzanne Buckingham Slade, 2013.

35. *Bigotry and Intolerance: The Ultimate Teen Guide,* by Kathlyn Gay, 2013.

36. *Substance Abuse: The Ultimate Teen Guide,* by Sheri Bestor, 2013.

37. *LGBTQ Families: The Ultimate Teen Guide,* by Eva Apelqvist, 2013.

38. *Bullying: The Ultimate Teen Guide,* by Mathangi Subramanian, 2014.

39. *Eating Disorders: The Ultimate Teen Guide,* by Jessica R. Greene, 2014.

40. *Speech and Language Challenges: The Ultimate Teen Guide,* by Marlene Targ Brill, 2014.

41. *Divorce: The Ultimate Teen Guide,* by Kathlyn Gay, 2014.

42. *Depression: The Ultimate Teen Guide,* by Tina P. Schwartz, 2014.

43. *Creativity: The Ultimate Teen Guide,* by Aryna Ryan, 2015.

44. *Shyness: The Ultimate Teen Guide,* by Bernardo J. Carducci, Ph.D, and Lisa Kaiser, 2015.

45. *Food Allergies: The Ultimate Teen Guide,* by Jessica Reino, 2015.

46. *Self-Injury: The Ultimate Teen Guide,* by Judy Dodge Cummings, 2015.

SELF-INJURY

THE ULTIMATE TEEN GUIDE

JUDY DODGE CUMMINGS

IT HAPPENED TO ME, NO. 46

ROWMAN & LITTLEFIELD
Lanham • Boulder • New York • London

Published by Rowman & Littlefield
A wholly owned subsidiary of The Rowman & Littlefield Publishing Group, Inc.
4501 Forbes Boulevard, Suite 200, Lanham, Maryland 20706
www.rowman.com

Unit A, Whitacre Mews, 26-34 Stannary Street, London SE11 4AB

British Library Cataloguing in Publication Information Available

Library of Congress Cataloging-in-Publication Data

Cummings, Judy Dodge.
  Self-injury : the ultimate teen guide / Judy Dodge Cummings.
    pages cm. — (It happened to me ; No. 46)
  Includes bibliographical references and index.
  ISBN 978-1-4422-4667-6 (hardback : alk. paper) — ISBN 978-1-4422-4668-3 (ebook)
 1. Self-mutilation in adolescence. 2. Cutting (Self-mutilation) 3. Self-destructive behavior in adolescence. I. Title.
  RJ506.S44C86 2015
  616.85'8200835—dc23
                                2015005551

∞™ The paper used in this publication meets the minimum requirements of American National Standard for Information Sciences—Permanence of Paper for Printed Library Materials, ANSI/NISO Z39.48-1992.

Printed in the United States of America

To young adults
everywhere who struggle
with addictive disorders.
May you find serenity and recovery.

Contents

Acknowledgments

I want to thank literary agent Jodell Sadler for steering this book opportunity in my direction and offering me support and advice throughout the process. Also, no book is finished until the keen eyes of a skilled editor have scrutinized it. Arlene Hirschfelder is such an editor. She is also insightful, kind, and patient. I appreciate her guidance throughout this project.

Introduction

It was a typical morning in my life as a high school teacher. About ten minutes before the first period bell rang, students began to filter into my classroom, some hyped up on caffeine, most sleepy-eyed. Sierra, a whip-thin senior girl with an unruly mane of brown hair, slumped down at the table in front of my desk.

"Good morning," I said. "How's it going?" This was my usual morning chatter.

But Sierra's response was not what I expected. "Last night sucked," she said quietly. The night before she had felt so awful that, in Sierra's words, she "had no choice but to cut again." She told me this matter-of-factly, as if carving up her body was simply her only option when life's pressures grew too great.

I am ashamed to say that I had no clue how to respond. I hemmed and hawed and mumbled something pathetic like "Cutting is not a very healthy way to handle things." Then I cleared my throat, looked anywhere but at Sierra, and started to teach my history class.

Later that day, I reported Sierra's remark to our school counselors. They knew of Sierra's emotional struggles and were in regular conversations with her. This knowledge relieved me, but the incident in the classroom haunted my mind for weeks. I cringed every time I thought about how Sierra had opened an inner door to her soul, and I had taken one look and slammed that door shut. During class I could not stop staring at her thin arms, covered in long sleeves regardless of the weather. Finally, I decided to do what I'm always preaching at my students to do—read.

As I read books and articles about self-injury, I recognized signs I had long ignored in my students. Emotions, behaviors, even clothing and jewelry choices can be a tip-off that someone is a self-injurer. I also learned that Sierra's story is not rare. A 2011 study found that one out of every twelve young people deliberately cuts, burns, or breaks her body in an attempt to feel better emotionally.[1] Due to the secret nature of this disorder, most experts believe the figure is actually much higher.[2]

The more I read about self-injury, the more the cycle of self-destructive behavior became disturbingly familiar to me. In my late teens and early twenties, I struggled with bulimia, the eating disorder in which people scarf down massive amounts of food and then purge it back out. Bulimia is a form of self-injury. Both bulimics and self-injurers experience a trigger event and the tension in their bodies rises until it becomes so unbearable that they must release it, either through binging and purging or by injuring. The relief this action brings is intense, but fleeting. Soon the individuals are filled with shame and self-loathing and the cycle begins again. Many young people who self-injure are also bulimic or anorexic. In Sierra's suffering, I saw the path my own life could have taken.

I wanted to write a book for Sierra and the millions of other young men and women like her; these young adults feel so alone and lonely, so angry and anxious, that they etch their pain into their flesh in the hopes of controlling it. If you self-harm, this book will let you know that you are not alone. Your struggle mirrors the struggles of many other young men and women. They have recovered, and you can too.

I also wanted to write a book for the friends and family of these troubled youth. Self-injury is terrifying for the people who love the individual wielding the razor or the lighter or the hammer. Most people assume that self-injury equates to suicide, but actually it signifies the opposite—people who self-harm are desperately trying to avoid suicide. If you are the parent or the best friend of someone who self-harms, the information in this book will educate you about self-injury disorder. Knowledge cannot cure your loved one's condition, but it can help ease your own anxiety. You will learn what you can and cannot control when it comes to caring for a person who self-harms.

Finally, I wanted to write this book for people like me—the teachers, coaches, employers, pastors, school nurses—the folks who interact with many young adults every day as part of their jobs. Young people enter our lives for a period of time, we get to know them and care about them, and then these youth move on again. If you work with young people, there is little doubt that you have interacted with a guy or girl who self-injures, but you might never have realized it, or you might have responded like I did—which is to say, without compassion or understanding. This book can teach you what signs to look for, what words to say, and how best to help.

In this book I define and describe the disorder of self-injury. As you will learn, people who harm themselves are not freaks or crazy. There is no one type of person who self-injures. Rich and poor, male and female, young and old, black and white—people from all walks of life harm their bodies. Each chapter features the stories of celebrities, singers and actors and artists who seem to have it all. But these famous personalities have more in common than fame and fortune. They also share a history of self-harm. Their stories demonstrate that this disorder strikes people whose lives may seem perfect to the rest of us.

For decades self-injury disorder remained hidden from the public eye. This has changed in the last twenty years. Now self-injury is a theme that runs through many novels, films, songs, and poetry. Each chapter will review several of these artistic expressions of self-harm in popular culture.

BEHIND THE SCAR

Skin is resilient. When it is damaged, it will fight to defend itself. Blood proteins work to create a scab. New tissue grows toward the center of the wound. If the injury was shallow, there will be no outward sign of damage when the body heals. But if the cut was deep, the body must work hard to protect itself. Deep wounds leave a scar—fibrous tissue that has no sweat glands, grows no hair, and is usually white.

A scar is a symbol. It tells the world that this person suffered an injury. But the scar does not reveal when the wound occurred. Or how. Or why. To get the answer to those questions you must go deeper—behind the scar.

Millions of young adults suffer from self-injury disorder. They hurt themselves on purpose, using their skin and flesh and bones as a kind of parchment to record stories of pain and loss and loneliness. Alicia and Luke are two such youth.

Emotional struggles lie behind a self-injurer's scars.

Alicia's Story

The metal edges of the torn soda can were razor sharp. Alicia Moore sliced it across her skin. She did it "almost on instinct,"[1] she said in recollection. She remembered looking down and "just having kind of this euphoric, everything's OK."[2]

At the time Alicia was only in the fifth grade.

As she grew older, the ripped soda can turned into razor blades, safety pins, scissors, broken CDs, anything with an edge sharp enough to break her skin. In her online diary, Alicia wrote, "Can't take the anger, can't take the pain. Must relieve the only way I can. Cut. Cut. Cut."[3]

On the outside Alicia looked like a girl with everything. She was a talented musician and dancer who earned high grades in school. But classmates teased her for these achievements and so she isolated herself. Alone and lonely, Alicia hurt herself to feel better. However, she was not suicidal. "I didn't cut myself to try to kill myself. I cut myself to release all of this emotional pain that I felt like I couldn't handle anymore."[4]

Luke's Story

At age fifteen Luke whipped his own back with a metal-tipped belt. Since that day he has bruised, scratched, cut, burned, stabbed, and suffocated himself. Luke's self-injury is compulsive. He must cut in multiples of fives and tens. But each time he cuts, he has an intense desire to ratchet the number higher. Instead of five cuts he will do ten. When he reaches thirty cuts, he will force himself to slice ten more times. "I made larger goals to 'achieve.' Get to 500. I believed I would stop when I achieved this, I did not stop. I am now aiming to do 1,000 cuts but already considering 1,500."[5]

Luke hurts himself because he feels so lonely. Even in a crowded room he feels alone. He wrote, "Loneliness eats away at you and takes away all the hope and happiness you have. Loneliness takes away your will to live. Even trying to get out of the bed is a challenge because it makes me afraid of the day to come."[6]

Alicia and Luke are just two examples in a sea of millions of American youth who self-injure. In order to understand why they do this, you must first understand what self-injury is.

A Definition of Self-Injury

The term *self-injury* might not sound very serious. After all, everyone injures themselves now and then. Who can resist tugging at a hangnail or popping a

Teen Voice: "Scars Tell a Story"

In an essay on the e-zine *Teen Ink*, a teen from Mead, Colorado, described what the scars of a self-injurer mean: "All scars tell a story. They tell a story of how they came to be." This youth cautioned that in order to understand the story behind the scar, you must be willing to see the pain, either emotional or physical, that self-injurers wear inside. She said, "I see scars differently than most because I have many on my body and in my heart. Even though some of my scars tell more of my story than others, they all make up part of my full story."[a]

pimple? It is common to bruise an elbow, bang a shin, or nick yourself while shaving. Most people do these things accidentally or subconsciously.

The disorder of self-injury is different. Slamming a hockey stick into your eye is not the same thing as kicking the sofa because you cannot find the remote. Self-injurers hurt themselves deliberately. They do not do this because they like pain. They injure themselves physically in order to escape or release emotional pain.[7]

Simply put, self-injury is a coping mechanism. Some people have healthy methods to manage stress—they run or meditate or pray. But many people use unhealthy ways of dealing with tough times. Alcohol, drugs, overeating, fighting—the list of ways people try to avoid pain is long. Although society does not like to talk about it, self-injury is another one of these methods of managing pain.

The Skin's Story

The skin is the body's largest organ. Adults carry around about eight pounds of skin that covers twenty-two feet. The skin guards the body against extreme heat and cold, damaging chemicals, and the harsh rays of sunlight. The skin sends out anti-bacteria to fight against infections, and it is packed with nerves. The deep layer of the skin known as the dermis is full of blood vessels and a network of nerve fibers that communicate pain and pleasure to the brain. For people who engage in self-injury the skin takes on one more role: it is the canvas on which they paint their pain.[b]

Self-injurers communicate their inner pain on the outside of their bodies.

One self-injurer described how she once cut herself sixteen times in one episode. As she stared at the red slashes that ran up and down her thigh, all she felt was "relief and euphoria. Relief because, despite the pain, it replaces every other pain. The sting is welcome; it makes me forget everything else."[8]

So in a nutshell, self-injury refers to the repeated and deliberate damage to body tissue as a means to avoid emotional pain. For Alicia and Luke the physical discomfort they inflicted on themselves was easier to endure than their feelings.

The Power of a Label

Examples of self-injury can be found in the historical record going back centuries; however, only in the last couple decades has the medical profession begun to seriously research this condition, and even today there is controversy over how to label it.

For a long time doctors who treated patients with self-inflicted wounds assumed these were unsuccessful suicide attempts so they called the behavior para-suicidal.[9] This label means "almost suicide" or "similar to suicide." Now mental health professionals know that people who self-injure are not trying to kill themselves. In fact, they are doing just the opposite. They are hurting themselves to release their emotional pain, which can act as a tool to *prevent* them from committing suicide.[10] The relationship between self-injury and suicide will be discussed more in chapter 3.

In the 1980s psychiatrists began to refer to the behavior they saw in their patients as self-mutilation. The word *mutilate* comes from the Latin word *mutilatus*. It means to maim. For decades self-injury was considered a symptom of borderline personality disorder, or BPD. Other symptoms of BPD include extreme mood swings, unstable relationships, and a distorted self-image.[11] People with BPD are often highly manipulative and crave attention. However, many self-injurers do not have these characteristics. Additionally, while there is a very small group of self-injurers, most of them severely mentally ill, who amputate their limbs or gouge out their eyes, these cases are rare. A man who punches a wall to release tension is not trying to permanently cripple himself. *Mutilation* is a harsh word and does not fully or accurately represent the millions of people who self-injure.

Some mental health and medical experts call this disorder nonsuicidal self-injury. This is an accurate label, but a cumbersome one. Others call it self-inflicted violence. However, the word *violence* implies that injury is the person's primary goal when what self-injurers are really seeking is relief.

A term used by popular magazines and newspapers to describe self-injury is *cutting*. While cutting with a sharp object is one of the most common methods of self-injury, using this term to represent all self-injury is misleading. People who self-harm use many methods, including ingesting poisons, burning themselves, and even breaking their own bones.

Today the term *self-injury* is used by both researchers and people in the mental health field who work with youth. Sociologists Peter and Patricia Adler have conducted extensive interviews with individuals who deliberately hurt themselves. They published their findings in a 2011 book titled *The Tender Cut*. The voices of self-injurers feature prominently in this book. The Adlers wanted to communicate how these people view their own behavior. The authors explained that "nearly all of these people regarded this behavior as a coping strategy, perhaps one they wished they did not need (and might someday be able to quit), but one that functioned to fill needs for them nevertheless."[12] The Adlers reported that most of the people they interviewed used the term *self-injury* to describe their own behavior, frequently referring to it by the abbreviation SI. One person called

Movie Review: Cut: Teens and Self-Injury, *Directed and Produced by Wendy Schneider, 2007*

In 2007 Wendy Schneider produced and directed the documentary *Cut: Teens and Self-Injury*. This film explores the emotions behind the wounds of self-injurers. There are no graphic depictions of cutting or burning. Instead, stories of pain are intimately revealed through interviews with young men and women. A mother and daughter pair offer dual perspectives on the cycle of emotion and isolation that fuels self-injury. Shirley Manson, the lead singer of the band Garbage, explains how music helped her recover. Two males are featured in the documentary, an important inclusion because the stereotype of the self-injurer as a white, teenage female is not accurate. The film showcases the art and writing of self-injurers in an effort to strip away some of the mystery behind what motivates people to hurt themselves.[c]

her self-harm "a friend." Another described is as "my own special thing."[13] Because the phrase *self-injury* is nonjudgmental, concise, and accurate, this label (or its acronym SI), will be used throughout this book to refer to the practice of deliberately damaging body tissue to alleviate emotional pain.

The Silent Epidemic

The newspaper headlines are alarming. They scream out that youth around the world are hurting themselves in epidemic proportions. While experts know that the number of young people who are self-injuring is on the rise, it is difficult for researchers to obtain a precise figure of how many people deliberately hurt themselves. Educational and advocacy groups claim that somewhere between two and three million Americans engage in self-injury.[14] These numbers come from reports from emergency rooms or clinics.[15] However, self-injury is a secret behavior. Most of the time people avoid seeking medical attention for their injuries. If they do go to the doctor, they fabricate stories of how they were hurt so health care providers fail to report the injury as self-inflicted.[16]

That was the case for Chrissy Tobias. This twenty-eight-year-old started cutting and banging her head against the wall when she was only twelve. But no

Musical Message: *"Bleed like Me"* by Garbage, Bleed like Me, Universal Music Group, 2005

Shirley Manson, the lead singer of the 1990s band Garbage, conveys powerful emotion through the lyrics of her music. The song "Bleed like Me" relates the pain of people who fight addictive behaviors and emotional pain. Avalanche is too thin, but never thin enough in her own mind. Chris wrestles with gender identity. Doodle uses her father's scissors to scar her skin in order to release her emotional pain. J. T. gets drunk. Shirley Manson echoes the plaintive cry of so many struggling youth when she sings, "Baby can you bleed like me?"[d]

one knew. She did well in school and was active in extracurricular activities, but when life became too stressful, Chrissy had an outlet. "I would typically use self-injury when things would get overwhelming, or when I felt like I had no outlet and had to do something about it . . . I would use it as a relief."[17] She did not seek help until she was twenty-one years old. So for years, Chrissy was not counted in the statistics that measure the number of people in the nation who self-harm. Imagine how many people like Chrissy exist. The true number of self-injurers is probably much higher than three million.

The most recent studies indicate that 1–4 percent of adults in the United States self-injure. Of these about 1 percent of them chronically self-harm.[18] However, among teens that number is higher. A 2005 study reported in the *Journal of Abnormal Psychology* found that 14–39 percent of American adolescents engage in self-injury.[19] That is a broad range. However, if you consider that there are about seventy million American youth, then even the lower figure of 14 percent means close to ten million youth deliberately hurt themselves. That means that you probably know a self-injurer. Or you are one yourself.

College students have been the focus of the latest research on self-injury. The largest study in the United States was conducted jointly by Princeton University and Cornell University in 2006. This study found that 17 percent of college students cut, carve, or burn their skin and break their bones. When divided by gender this translates to 20 percent of female college students and 14 percent of males who deliberate hurt themselves physically in order to cope emotionally. Another disturbing statistic is that of these students, only 7 percent sought medical help for their injuries.[20] These young men and women are suffering in secret.

Answers and Assistance

In 2003 Cornell University started a program to research what they believed was a new and dangerous trend in the behavior of young people—self-injury. In the years since, researchers with the Cornell Research Program on Self-Injury and Recovery (CRPSIR) have been involved in multiple projects to try to better understand the causes of SI and how to treat it. They periodically seek self-injuring youth or their parents to participate in research studies. Additionally, CRPSIR works to translate research into user-friendly materials for self-injurers and those who care about them. The website for this organization can be found at http://www.selfinjury.bctr.cornell.edu/. There you will find a blog, links to academic resources, and helpful books and articles, as well as video clips that explore topics from symptoms to recovery.[e]

The average age when people commit their first act of self-injury is between fourteen and fifteen, but self-injury is not just a disorder of early adolescence. More than 41 percent of the students in the Cornell study first injured themselves between the ages of seventeen and twenty-two. That means they began to self-injure while in college. More than three-fourths of these students hurt themselves more than once, and 70 percent used more than one method to wound their bodies.[21]

While the injuries may start out minor, they often escalate. As a thirteen-year-old girl wrote in an online forum, "everyone says self harming gets better but mine only seems to be getting worse. For example, bigger urges = harder to control = bigger cuts."[22] Statistics back up her words. One-fifth of the students in the Cornell study reported that they had hurt themselves more severely than they had intended at least once. A quarter of them said that their injuries were bad enough to have seen a doctor, but most did not seek medical help.[23]

For a long time self-injury was a taboo topic. Sufferers did not admit that they abused their bodies. Parents were oblivious to what their children were doing. The media, educators, and the medical profession were either unaware of the disorder or dismissed it as teenagers just seeking attention. Then in the 1980s and 1990s a few celebrities publicly revealed that they had injured themselves. These

---

Celebrity Spotlight: Shirley Manson

Shirley Manson, the red-haired Scottish lead singer of the band Garbage, stopped cutting herself years ago, but still calls herself a cutter. From the time she was twelve or thirteen, she carried sharp objects in the laces of her boots and cut herself when she felt overwhelmed by anxiety or depression. Joining a band and expressing her feelings through music enabled Manson to stop self-injury, although she still gets urges.[f]

In a 2012 interview Manson was asked if she still cut. She replied, "I don't physically cut, no, but I psychologically cut myself on a regular basis. Or at least I did up until when my mum died." After her mother's death in 2008, Manson had an awakening. "I was, like: 'Why are you attacking yourself constantly?' It's such a stupid waste of time. I was, like: 'You need to sober up; you need to grow up and take responsibility.'"[g]

---

confessions, coupled with landmark work by key researchers, finally brought the wounds of sufferers into the light.

The best way to understand self-injury disorder is to listen to the voices of the people who self-harm. This book is full of their stories. One teen posted anonymously on the e-zine *Teen Ink*. Her words urge us to pay attention.

> I am a self harmer. Or, at least I was. I've been clean for 6 months and I've sworn to never do it again. But, I suppose what they say is true, that the urge never leaves you. It's a clawed demon, constantly trying to escape and you have to constantly fight to push it down, deep within your soul. . . . Do me the honor of listening for a few minutes; who knows, maybe you will actually learn something.[24]

Let us do what this young woman asks: listen, learn, and understand.

Wrap-Up

Now you know that self-injury is a disorder known by many names. Despite what it is labeled, people who use this coping mechanism have the same goal: they

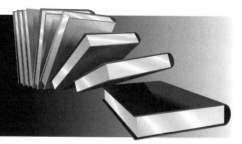

Read about It: Two or Three Things I Forgot to Tell You *(New York: HarperCollins, 2014)*

The novel *Two or Three Things I Forgot to Tell You* by Joyce Carol Oates is the story of two friends—Merissa, the Perfect One, and Nadia, the Slut. Their friend Tink committed suicide at the end of their junior year of high school. Both Merissa and Nadia have been struggling since Tink's death. Merissa cuts herself to escape the pressure of being perfect enough to earn her father's love. Nadia wants someone, anyone, to love her. Her mother is dead, her father ignores her, and her stepmother is cruel so Nadia develops an obsessive crush on her science teacher and tries to starve herself into beauty. Ultimately, memories of Tink help both girls find their way to self-acceptance and recovery.

hurt their bodies to escape their emotional pain. While we do not know exactly how many people in the United States have self-injury disorder, they number in the millions and often suffer in secret. Chapter 2 will explore the history of this mental illness from its ancient past to the present.

FROM CRAZY TO CULT– HOW PERSPECTIVES OF SELF-INJURY HAVE EVOLVED

If you self-injure, you probably do so in secret. You may believe that you are the only person in the world with this problem. Far from it. Millions of people around the world harm their bodies for emotional reasons, and SI has been recorded throughout human history. To understand the present nature of this disorder, we will begin with the past. The perception and treatment of self-injury has evolved throughout the centuries. Once considered a behavior only practiced by seriously mentally ill patients, today some people call SI a fad, others an epidemic.

Ancient Times to the Twentieth Century

Trauma causes emotional stress. Some people try to escape this stress through self-injury. Few experiences are more traumatic than fighting on the battlefield. Today a veteran who experiences flashbacks, crippling fear, and paranoia would be diagnosed and treated for post-traumatic stress disorder. Warriors in the ancient world did not benefit from such a diagnosis.

Herodotus lived in Greece during the fifth century BCE. He is considered "the father of history" because he systematically collected and organized historical data. Herodotus wrote a multivolume account of the Greek and Persian wars, and in one of the volumes he reported a graphic account of self-injury.

Cleomenes was king of Sparta from 520 to 490 BCE. He led the Greeks in war against the Persian Empire and also battled takeover attempts by his own relatives. Years of fighting for his life and throne caused Cleomenes to mentally disintegrate. His behavior became bizarre. Whenever he met someone, he jabbed the person in the face with his scepter. His relatives ordered Cleomenes impris-

The first recorded incidence of self-injury dates back to the fifth century BCE.

oned and kept his feet locked in stocks. One day when only a slave stood guard over him, Cleomenes ordered the man to turn over his knife. Cleomenes was still technically the king of Sparta and the slave was terrified of what might happen if he did not obey. So the slave handed Cleomenes his knife. The king did not try to escape. Instead he used the knife to carve up his own body. Herodotus described Cleomenes "cutting gashes in his flesh, along his legs, thighs, hips, and loins, until at last he reached his belly, which he likewise began to gash, whereupon in a little time he died."[1] The Spartan king's self-mutilation is the earliest written record of self-injury and was probably the result of a severe mental illness.

During the Middle Ages, many people self-injured as part of extreme religious rituals. The Black Death was a plague that swept through Europe in the mid-fourteenth century. Many people believed that God had sent the fatal disease

Two Flagellants flogging themselves during an epidemic in Europe in the Middle Ages.

to punish them. A group of Christians called the Flagellants whipped themselves to atone for their sins. White-robed Flagellants carried crosses and marched by the thousands through the countryside of Europe. Each man whipped the back of the man in front of him with a three-pronged whip. Sir Robert of Avesbury witnessed a group who marched on London in 1349 and he recorded the scene: "Each had in his right hand a scourge with three tails. Each tail had a knot and through the middle of it there were sometimes sharp nails fixed. They marched naked in a file one behind the other and whipped themselves with these scourges on their naked and bleeding bodies."[2]

It was not just men who abused their bodies in an attempt to achieve spiritual purity. In the 1300s, the parents of Catherine of Sienna pressured her to marry her dead sister's widower. However, Catherine saw herself as a bride of Christ and refused to marry. She cut off her long hair, put iron chains on her waist, dressed in a rough woolen shift, and survived on a diet of bread, water, raw vegetables, and bitter herbs. Three times daily she whipped herself with a chain. Catherine joined a religious order of nuns and devoted her life to working with the poor. After a lengthy fast from all food and water, she died at the age of thirty-three.[3]

She was eventually declared a saint by the Catholic Church. Catherine was one of many Christian women in the Middle Ages who believed that the path to salvation lay through self-injury. At this time in history, abusing one's body was admired as a sign of religious devotion.

People pay more attention to extreme behaviors. The historical record is full of cases of people with severe mental illnesses who brutalized their bodies in unimaginable ways. For example, in 1851 as a woman was feverishly reading the Bible, she reached the book of Matthew, chapter 5, verse 29. There it is written, "If your right eye causes you to sin, gouge it out and throw it away."[4] When the woman read these instructions, she dug her own eyeball out with a meat hook. This horrific scene was not an isolated example of self-destruction. In 1887, a twenty-nine-year-old man was quietly reading a book when he reached down and yanked off his scrotum. He then handed it to his mother and told her to take it because he did not want it anymore.[5] There are many other similarly gruesome examples that are peppered here and there in the records of mental institutions.

Then at the end of the nineteenth century, New York doctors George Gould and Walter Pyle reported on a bizarre form of self-injury that took on an almost fad-like quality. Women across western Europe punctured themselves with needles. The press called them the "needle girls." One woman had 217 needles removed from her body over an eighteen-month period. Another woman killed

The Case of Helen Miller

In July 1875, Helen Miller was admitted to the State Asylum for Insane Criminals in Auburn, New York. She had been serving time for theft at Sing Sing prison but after she began to injure herself, she was transferred to the mental hospital. Miller was thirty years old. Her doctor, Walter Channing, recounted the severe damage Miller inflicted on her body. The first time he treated her, she broke twenty-three panes of glass, sliced herself, and inserted glass into her wounds. Eventually she calmed down and her wounds were stitched up. This behavior became Miller's pattern. Dr. Channing listed the items that he removed from Miller's body throughout the eighteen months that she was his patient: ninety-four pieces of glass, thirty-four splinters, two tacks, four shoe nails, one pin, and one needle. The longest splinter was almost six inches long. Miller claimed that she felt no pain when she injured herself.[a]

herself by inserting pins into her skin and then slowly pressing them into her heart by pressing a Bible against her chest.[6] These needle girls were women who were either incarcerated or in mental institutions.

Self-Harm Is Not Suicide

For many years, mental health professionals believed SI was a failed suicide attempt. The first person to formally challenge this assumption was Dr. Karl Menninger in 1938. He coined the term *self-mutilation* to refer to SI, and he said suicide and mutilation were two different psychological problems. Menninger maintained that patients who self-injured were not trying to kill themselves. Rather, they were sacrificing part of their body in order to maintain their whole self. The abuse of the body was a result of conflicting urges within a person—the desire to destroy oneself and the will to survive. Menninger believed that self-injury satisfied the

Menninger's Mark

Mentally ill patients used to be treated like animals. They were housed in prisons, kept in chains, and beaten and abused. Conditions began to improve in the twentieth century. Karl Menninger was at the forefront of this improvement. Menninger was born in Topeka, Kansas, in 1893. He studied neuropathology at Harvard before returning to Kansas to open up a clinic with his brother and father. Karl Menninger refused to classify patients into rigid categories of illnesses. He believed that most people struggling with emotional problems would respond positively to a loving, caring environment. Menninger also insisted that some of his patients' troubles did not come from their minds, but rather their environments, especially their parents.

Menninger's first book, *The Human Mind*, was published in 1930. Although it was intended for medical students, the book became popular with the public. In *The Human Mind*, Menninger argued that people with mental illnesses must be treated humanely rather than locked up as lunatics. This book was an important step in changing people's perceptions about how society should care for people with mental illnesses. In 1981 Menninger received the Medal of Freedom from President Jimmy Carter. He died in 1990 at the age of 96.[b]

need to hurt while actually preventing suicide since the hurt inflicted was deliber-ately not fatal.[7]

Slow Progress: 1960s–1980s

In the 1960s, a rise in the number of self-injury patients resulted in a brief burst of attention from mental health researchers. By this time some in the academic community had begun to distinguish self-injury from suicide, but most clinic and hospital staff still treated patients who came in with self-inflicted wounds as suicide risks. Two doctors in Philadelphia, Harold Graff and Richard Mallin, saw a large influx of women who came into their psychiatric hospital with slashes to their wrists. These patients were labeled as suicidal, but Graff and Mallin dis-agreed. They collected data and looked for common characteristics among these women. They used six months of admissions records and developed the following profile of a self-injurer: intelligent, young, and female; prone to alcohol and other drug addictions; a history of sexual abuse or other trauma in their backgrounds; a cold, distant mother and an aloof, overly critical father.[8]

At the same time, another team of psychiatrists, Henry Grunebaum and Ger-ald Klerman, saw a similar pattern at their mental hospital in Massachusetts. In 1967 the pair published their conclusions in the *American Journal of Psychiatry*. They also laid blame on the parents of SI patients. Grunebaum and Klerman said that the women they treated had backgrounds full of physical and sexual abuse. Their fathers were drunks and molested them; their mothers were cold and rejected them. The women cut themselves as a way to release their negative emotions. One patient described cutting herself this way: "It's like vomiting. You feel sick and spit out the badness."[9] These reports were an important beginning. Some experts in the mental health field recognized that patients who self-injured shared distinct characteristics that did not always match up with other disorders.

However, this brief surge of attention from researchers died down quickly. A few studies were conducted in the 1970s, but little changed in diagnosis and treatment of SI patients. They were frequently misdiagnosed as suicidal or their self-injury was seen as just one symptom of a more serious mental illness.

One of the flaws in the data during this time in history was that all the aca-demic studies on SI had been conducted on people who were in mental hospital facilities. Therefore, the results of this early research were skewed. Researchers had no understanding about the degree of self-injury among the larger population of people who did not seek medical help and were not housed in mental health institutions. Then in the 1980s, the work of Dr. Armando Favazza began to fill in these gaps in our knowledge of SI.

Favazza worked in the field of cultural psychiatry. He studied how mental illnesses interconnect to a person's cultural background. In 1980 Favazza was

Movie Review: Girl Interrupted, *Directed by James Mangold, Columbia Pictures, 1999*

After swallowing a bottle of aspirin followed by a quart of vodka, Susanna Kaysen is diagnosed with borderline personality disorder and committed to an upscale private mental hospital where she gets to know a group of women struggling with demons worse than her own. Daisy only eats the rotisserie chicken that her father delivers to her. She saves the chicken bones under her bed and is addicted to laxatives. Polly is disfigured from a burn inflicted by her father, and Lisa is a sociopath. When Lisa pushes up the sleeve of Daisy's robe to reveal a patchwork of scars, Daisy tells Lisa to look at her own wrists. Lisa replies, "I'm sick. We know that, but here you are in recovery playing Betty Crocker cut up like a . . . Virginia ham."

Daisy's tragic end is just one of a series of stories based on this true-to-life film based on Susan Kaysen's memoir by the same title. She actually spent eighteen months in a mental hospital in the 1960s. This film is raw and hard to watch. The actors' performances are brilliantly troubling. The movie portrays a panorama of mental illnesses and the human faces of the women who struggle to overcome them.

---

consulted by a colleague about a depressed patient who slashed herself with razor blades. This doctor wanted Favazza's expertise on how self-injury shows up in cultures outside the United States; however, Favazza discovered that he knew very little about the topic. "I went to my file cabinet, but the folder on self-mutilation was thin and not very helpful."[10] So he consulted other experts on cultural psychiatry, but no one knew much about this disorder. Next Favazza went to the library. However, he could not find a single academic book that examined self-injury across cultures. At that point Favazza realized that if he wanted to learn about SI, he was going to have to conduct the research himself.

First, Favazza analyzed some literature he had uncovered about North African Islamic healers. These men prayed so frenetically that they worked themselves into frenzies and slashed their skin. Sugar cubes were then dipped into the healers' blood and fed to the sick patients. Favazza realized that the self-injury of these healers was aimed at helping people recover. He considered this fact alongside

Menninger's earlier work that had concluded that patients who self-injured did so in order to avoid committing suicide. Then Favazza set about comparing the methods and meaning of self-injury in cultures throughout history and across the world. His research was broad, covering mutilation for decorative purposes, in religious rituals, and due to psychological disorders.[11]

After being rejected by several publishers because the topic of the book was too "disgusting," Favazza's book *Bodies under Siege* was published in 1987. In the preface, he explains that he wanted to "strip away the mysterious aura that surrounds self-mutilation."[12] He takes a no-holds-barred approach as he traces the meaning of self-injury across cultures and over distinct historical eras. Much of Favazza's analysis is of self-harm done as part of cultural rituals. For example, the Gazing-at-the-Sun Dance ceremony was a traditional practice among the

Read about It: The Bell Jar (New York: Harper & Row, 1971)

The Bell Jar, by Sylvia Plath, is a semiautobiographical novel about depression and mental illness. Esther is a small-town girl in New York City on a scholarship. The book chronicles her struggles with men and her consistently thwarted efforts to make it as a writer. But the heart of this story is Esther's descent into madness. She stops sleeping. She doesn't bathe. She can't read or write. Finally, Esther sees a psychiatrist, and when talk therapy does not lift Esther's depression, she receives what was standard treatment protocol in the 1960s—electric shock therapy. Two metal straps are fitted to each side of her head, and she is given a metal wire to bite down on. Then, "Whee-ee-ee-ee, it shrilled, through an air crackling with blue light, and with each flash a great jolt drubbed me till I thought my bones would break and the sap fly out of me like a split plant."[c]

Esther would receive more shocks over the course of her numerous treatments to battle her depression. She contemplates suicide, making experimental slashes on her legs to test her will. "Then I felt a small, deep thrill, and a bright seam of red welled up at the lip of the slash. The blood gathered darkly, like fruit, and rolled down my ankle into the cup of my black patent leather shoe."[d] This book is a very emotional read, even more so because its author, Sylvia Plath, committed suicide in 1963.

buffalo hunting Indian tribes of the Arapahoe, Cheyanne, and Dakota. Men volunteered for this painful performance, but the entire tribe both cooperated in and was believed to benefit from their sacrifice. As women sang grief songs, the volunteers inserted leather thongs into the muscles of their chests. These thongs were then attached to the Sacred Pole and the dancers were lifted off the ground as they gazed at the sun. For some men, the pain was too much and they had to be cut down. Others struggled until the leather broke through their skin and they fell to the ground. If the dancer was pure of heart, members of the tribe believed, he would receive a vision after the ceremony to help guide his path through life.[13] There are scores of other examples of ritualistic self-harm in Favazza's research. He explores how religious beliefs and self-injury interconnect in both indigenous religions and the monotheistic faiths, most specifically Christianity.

Favazza analyzed the meaning these rituals held for different cultures and he broadened the definition of self-injury. He divided the disorder into four main categories, which will be discussed in the next chapter.[14] The publication of *Bodies under Siege* signaled a major change in the conversation about self-injury. No longer would SI be seen as a condition from which only the extremely disturbed suffered. Nor would it be an illness discussed only among academics and doctors. Self-injury was about to emerge from the shadows.

1990s through Early Twenty-First Century

Despite the positive reviews that *Bodies under Siege* received when it was published, academic literature alone was not enough to change the global conversation about self-injury. It would take a princess to do that.

In 1995, Princess Diana, wife of Prince Charles, the heir to the British throne, revealed in a television interview that she had self-harmed. And Diana was not the only star to confess to such behavior. Other celebrities—including Fiona Apple, Angelina Jolie, Courtney Love, Johnny Depp, Marilyn Manson, and others—told similar stories. Television programs in the late 1990s such as *ER* and *The Guardian* included self-injury in their plotlines. Gradually, the public became aware of how widespread this disorder was, although what caused it or why people would intentionally hurt themselves remained a mystery.[15]

In the midst of the media blitz about celebrity self-harm, two journalists wrote accounts of the disorder that exposed the public to the very ordinary face of people who hurt themselves. In July of 1997 the first story made the cover of one of the most widely read magazines in the nation—the *New York Times Magazine*. It was written by Jennifer Egan and titled "The Thin Red Line."

Egan shadowed Jill, a tall, blonde, outwardly confident, sixteen-year-old from Chicago. While on the outside Jill was popular and in control, inside she was a mess. Jill felt such intense anxiety, self-doubt, and shame that at the age

Public awareness grew when celebrities revealed that they had self-injured.

Celebrity Spotlight: Princess Diana

In 1980, nineteen-year-old Diana Spencer married Prince Charles. She was unprepared for the intense public scrutiny that life as a member of the British royal family would bring. Diana was tall, blonde, and beautiful, and she connected with common people in a way that few in the British royal family ever had. Her charisma and sensitivity earned her the title of the "people's princess."

However, Diana also had a darker side. According to biographer Sally Bedell Smith, Diana bore the classic markings of someone with a borderline personality disorder. In *Diana in Search of Herself: Portrait of a Troubled Princess*, Smith interviewed friends and family and palace staff who described Diana's wild mood swings. She feared abandonment and was impulsive and often depressed.[e] She could not stop reading news and gossip reports about herself. If they were favorable, she was elated. If they were critical, she hated herself. As the pressures of palace life grew, Diana sought relief through self-injury. In a 1995 interview she said,

> You have so much pain inside yourself that you try and hurt yourself on the outside because you want help. . . . People see it as crying wolf or attention-seeking, . . . but I was actually crying out because I wanted to get better in order to go forward and continue my duty and my role as wife, mother, Princess of Wales. . . . So yes, I did inflict upon myself. I didn't like myself, I was ashamed because I couldn't cope with the pressures.[f]

In addition to injuring her body, Diana was also bulimic for more than three years.

Princess Diana was one of the first celebrities to speak openly about her struggles with self-injury. She was beloved by many people and perhaps could have served for a role model to women who struggled with self-harm. However, Diana did not have a chance to reach such potential. She was killed in 1996 when the driver of her limousine, drunk at the time, was attempting to flee a herd of paparazzi and hit a concrete embankment.

of fourteen she sliced herself with a wallpaper cutter. This act provided relief and Jill was hooked.[16]

Egan's article painted a different portrayal of self-injurers than those previously described in accounts of mental health professionals. In addition to Jill, Egan interviewed a college student, Jamie, and a business woman named Jane. Although they began to self-injure at different times in their lives and for different reasons, self-injury helped all three women cope with emotional stress. "The Thin Red Line" reached a large audience and told the story of self-injury as it affected seemingly ordinary families.[17]

Then in 1998, *A Bright Red Scream* hit the bookstores. Journalist Marilee Strong interviewed dozens of people and wrote a compassionate and informative book. Her detailed case studies reveal how complicated self-injury disorder is. The men and women whom Strong interviewed came from a variety of backgrounds; some were teenagers and others grandmothers. Some had been abused as children; others came from loving, intact families. The tone of *A Bright Red Scream* is not clinical or academic. Strong is a storyteller and the way she relates the struggles of self-injurers is sensitive and gripping. For example, Strong opens the book with an email from a self-injurer named Andrew. He writes,

> It's that feeling again. You wake up and see blood stains on your sheets and on your carpet. Books and bits of paper strewn all over your room. Broken furniture. The familiar sting on your arms and your torso. Your face is smeared red. You were doing so well too—thirteen days since the last time.

Musical Message: "Breathe Me," by Sia Furler, Colour the Small One, Universal Records, 2004

"Breathe Me" is a breathless, heartrending lament by Australian pop artist Sia Furler. She said the song was "about feeling worried, generally anxious. Being overwhelmed by your own inner dialogue and having some sort of conniption fit and potentially doing yourself some harm, then asking for help." In fact, the very first word of the song is "help." Regret is palpable when Furler sings that she has hurt herself again, "lost myself and I am nowhere to be found." Regardless of what form self-injury takes or what causes a person to self-harm, following the act there is inevitable remorse and shame about the behavior.[9]

You feel numb, dazed, hung-over, stupid. You can hardly get yourself up. You haven't eaten for three days, and you've lost a lot of blood. Just what are you trying to prove?[18]

Andrew is just one of scores of self-injurers featured in *A Bright Red Scream*. Strong explores different psychological theories for what causes self-injury, and she illuminates these explanations with detailed accounts drawn from the lives of real people. The media and the public paid attention to Strong's work and researchers followed suit. Mental health professionals began to look outside the doors of hospitals and mental institutions and quickly discovered that the number of self-injurers and the kind of people who self-injured were far more complex than anyone had realized before.

Self-Injury in the Twenty-First Century

The onset of the twenty-first century brought a transformation in our perception of self-injury. The Internet reduced the isolation of self-injurers. Websites devoted to SI sprang up. Chat rooms allowed people to interact with self-injurers and those who had recovered from the disorder. Sociologists Patricia and Peter Adler examined SI in the context of the digital age. When *The Tender Cut* was published in 2011, it was different from the pivotal works of the previous two decades. This book was the first major academic study to examine the hidden population of self-injurers including long-term injurers, middle-aged populations, minorities, the homeless, and people in the military. The Adlers' extensive interviews and analysis of tens of thousands of Internet messages and emails resulted in their conclusion that "Self-injury has become demedicalized in its practice, changing from being primarily a medical disorder, or a disease, into a social trend."[19] For example, youth who identify as emo and goth engage in self-injury to express their rejection of society or to claim membership in these subcultures. The Adlers argue that as self-injury expanded, it "took on new social meanings, remaining a behavior practiced by psychologically troubled individuals, who used it to soothe their trauma, but it also became a legitimate mode of emotional expression and relief among a much wider population."[20] The Internet and social media has fueled the spread of SI. This topic will be explored in chapter 6.

The Adlers selected the title of their book, *The Tender Cut*, with great care. They acknowledge that "it may seem oxymoronic to refer to cutting oneself intentionally as tender. By this term we intend to convey what the individuals we studied thought about this behavior, which was accepting."[21] People who self-harm hurt themselves in order to help themselves. This contradiction will be explored much more throughout the rest of this book.

Self-Embedders

The practice of self-injury continues to change, as does our understanding of it. In 2008 North American radiologists gathered for their annual meeting during which evidence of a disturbing new trend was shared. Dr. William Shiels, chief of radiology at Nationwide Children's Hospital in Columbus, Ohio, showed X-rays of eleven patients that came to his office to have objects removed from their bodies. He performed a surgical procedure on them that he usually uses to remove shrapnel from soldiers. Shiels called these teenagers "self-embedders." From their bodies he removed items including an eight-centimeter bobby pin, three staples, chunks of pencil lead, and glass and wood shards that were lodged in forearms. One youth had taken two large paper clips, unfolded them, and inserted each seven-inch length of metal into his biceps. Other teens had sliced open their skin and implanted safety pins or chunks of crayon in their arms, ankles, necks. Although all forms of self-injury are dangerous, self-embedding has particular risks. Muscle and bone infections are possible. An artery, vein, nerve, or tendon can be damaged. Also objects can travel once they are inside the body, even approaching vital organs.[22]

The main difference Dr. Shiels found between embedding and other types of self-injury is the mental health of the patient. Shiels said that "with self-embedding behavior we see more severe behavioral health abnormalities."[23] These include bipolar disorder, depression, and post-traumatic stress disorder. Another difference is that while most self-injury is done to obtain relief or to feel better, people who self-embed seem more intent on hurting themselves. Dr. Shiels's study found that 90 percent of self-embedders had considered suicide.[24]

Because this extreme form of self-injury has only recently come on the radar of mental health experts, there is no data about how widespread the problem is. Dr. Shiels wants to set up a national registry to track cases of self-embedding so doctors can gauge the scope of the problem. Professor Nancy Heath from McGill University believes that self-embedding "is definitely a phenomenon that is out there that exists."[25] She maintains that anyone who self-harms should be assessed for suicide risk, but a self-embedding should be given a full psychiatric evaluation as well.

Present Status of Self-Injury Disorder

The silent epidemic is no longer silent. Self-injury is a theme in young adult novels and movies and music. This disorder is being researched by academics, recognized by medical professionals, and treated by mental health workers.

Answers and Assistance

Self Abuse Finally Ends (S.A.F.E.) Alternatives is a treatment philosophy that started in 1986. It is rooted in the belief that although self-injury might temporarily help someone feel better, it is ultimately a self-destructive act. Therapists who follow the S.A.F.E. Alternatives model strive to empower individuals. They help patients delay the urge to self-harm so that they have time to use alternative means of coping with their emotions. S.A.F.E. Alternatives runs adult and adolescent inpatient intensive treatment programs as well as short outpatient programs. People who cannot access one of the facilities can go to the S.A.F.E. Alternatives website (http://www.selfinjury.com/) and use its therapist referral service to find a mental health counselor in their community. This website has links to the newest research about SI and a blog where people can post their personal experiences.[h]

The *Diagnostic and Statistical Manual of Mental Disorders* (*DSM*) is the book mental health professionals rely on to classify, diagnose, and treat patients. It has been used since the early 1950s. In 2013 the *DSM-5* (fifth edition) listed Nonsuicidal Self-Injury (NSSI) as a distinct condition for the first time in history. Previously, it was only considered to be a symptom of borderline personality disorder. Researchers have finally acknowledged that self-injury occurs in patients who have no other identifiable mental illnesses. To be considered to have NSSI, a person must have five or more days of injury to the surface of the body without suicidal intent. The inclusion of NSSI in this manual of mental illness is an important step in the diagnosis, research, and treatment of people who suffer from self-injury. [26]

Wrap-Up

Self-injury disorder has existed throughout human history. Prior to the twentieth century, the disorder was regarded as either a sign of severe mental disturbance or extreme religious devotion. Our understanding has evolved. Today most mental health professionals realize that SI is not a failed suicide attempt, and the disorder can appear in people who do not have any other mental illnesses. However, despite the increased awareness of SI, there is still much stigma associated with this disorder. Many people react with fear and disgust when confronted with self-injury. Knowledge will help reduce that stigma. In the next chapter we will explore who self-injures and how they do so.

BLADES, BURNS, AND BONES

My son has nine tattoos on his body. Some are so small as to be barely visible, but one covers his chest. It took six hours for the artist to burn the tattoo into my son's skin. One of my students has large plug holes in her earlobes, a pierced tongue, and a belly button ring. My sister-in-law had a tummy tuck. After the procedure, she could barely sit up for a week. These are some examples of how people harm themselves in socially acceptable ways.

Tattoos, body piercings, and plastic surgery are not symptoms of self-injury disorder. Sometimes it helps to understand what a disorder is by first examining what it is not.

 Self-Injury Quiz

Take this quiz to see how much you know about self-injury. Are these statements true or false?

- Incidences of self-injury are very rare.
- Only people with mental illnesses commit self-injury.
- People who self-injure do so in order to get attention.
- Self-injury is very rare among males.
- The only way to help people who self-injure is to put them in a hospital.

Every answer is false. How did you do? Read on and you'll learn more about the true nature of self-injury disorder.

Tattooing one's body for decorative purposes is not self-injury disorder.

Practices That Are Not Self-Injury Disorder

Cultural Rituals and Gender Roles

People in societies around the world pierce, tattoo, and scar their bodies, and they have done so throughout history. In 1991, climbers in the Alps discovered the frozen remains of a Bronze Age man. Fifty tattoos marked his 5,300-year-old corpse. These tattoos were made by slicing the skin and then rubbing charcoal over the wound. Because the tattoos mark the prehistoric man's joints and back, areas prone to injury, anthropologists believe this scarification represents an early form of acupuncture.[1]

Today tattoos can be a rite of passage for some young adults and a fashion statement for others. According to a 2012 Harris Poll, one in five Americans has at least one tattoo, a rate that has steadily risen over the last decade. People reported tattoos made them feel sexier, stronger, rebellious, smarter, and more spiritual. Tattoos are designed to be shown to the world.[2] They are not a symptom of self-injury disorder, an illness cloaked in shame and secrecy.

Tattoos are not the only type of body modification that is a reflection of culture rather than a sign of mental illness. For centuries, Chinese girls had their feet bound. Between the ages of three and seven, all toes, except the big one, would be broken and pressed back against the bottom of the foot. Bandages were wound around the foot to maintain the pressure and force the foot to grow in this stunted fashion. Men reputedly found the swaying, swishing walk of women with bound feet erotic. This degree of severe restriction of the body was not limited to Chinese culture. During the Victorian Age in the late nineteenth century, Western women wore corsets cinched so tightly that they acted like a rib cage, and women's internal organs shifted to adapt to this hourglass shape. Women aspired to have waists of twelve inches.[3] While certainly disfiguring and painful, bound feet and corseted waists reveal a culture's gender roles. They are not examples of self-injury disorder.

Societal expectations about physical appearance still pressures people, women especially, to strive for perfection. In 2013, plastic surgeons in the United States performed 14.6 million cosmetic surgery procedures. This rate was 5 percent higher than in 2011.[4] Lift the eyelids. Tuck the tummy. Enlarge the breasts. Smooth out the wrinkles. Every day women willingly place themselves in the hands of a doctor armed with a scalpel who is intent on carving their bodies. For most people, cosmetic surgery is about improving one's physical appearance—like dieting or changing your hair color. The goal is not to regulate your emotions. For most people, the behavior is not addictive; therefore, cosmetic surgery is not self-injury.

In some cultures there is power and purpose to self-injury. In Singapore devoted Hindus commemorate the festival of Thaipusam by carrying heavy spiked cages over a long distance after days of fasting. Although the spikes pierce their chests and torso, the people endure the pain because this ritual is done as either an act of penance or one of thanksgiving.[5] In the United States today about 77 percent of parents have their newborn sons circumcised, some as a preventive medical measure and others for cultural or religious reasons.[6] For followers of Judaism, for example, circumcision is a commandment handed down by God.

According to the Torah, a sacred text of the Jewish religion, God told his follower Abraham that all male infants must be circumcised on the eighth day of their lives. Jews believe that the removal of the foreskin that surrounds the male penis is a symbol that represents God's sacred bond with the Jewish people.

Cosmetic Surgery Can Be Addictive for Some

When Steve Erhardt moved from rural Pennsylvania to Beverly Hills, California, he entered the land of the beautiful. Working in an upscale salon, Steve wanted to be beautiful too. Thirty-seven cosmetic procedures and $250,000 later, he is still trying to achieve a beauty that seems forever out of reach. Steve is an example of someone with body dysmorphic disorder. No matter what they look like on the outside, people with this disorder always feel ugly. They starve themselves or undergo scores of chemical or surgical procedures in an effort to feel better about themselves. While this disorder affects 1–3 percent of Americans, up to 15 percent of people who undergo cosmetic surgery are reputed to have it. Body dysmorphic disorder is not self-injury disorder, but the two conditions share similar patterns: emotional need, abuse of the body, and addiction.[a]

Abraham lived around 2000 BCE, a time when people believed in the existence of many gods. Judaism was the first monotheistic, or one-god, religion. Rituals such as circumcision helped the Jews maintain their religious and cultural identity through centuries of persecution.

In the Brit Milah ceremony, the newborn boy is welcomed by a prayer and a hymn from the congregation. Then the religious leader or rabbi amputates the foreskin with one clean sweep of a knife. The blood is quickly swabbed or suctioned away, and then the rabbi blesses the child and pronounces his name. A feast and more prayers and songs follow.[7]

Tattoos, piercings, and circumcision are examples of body injury that are socially sanctioned. They are done for a purpose that society has deemed acceptable—beauty, religion, tradition. While body tissue is damaged, these procedures are not attempts to eliminate emotional stress; therefore, they are not symptoms of self-injury disorder. According to Tracy Alderman, author of *The Scarred Soul: Understanding and Ending Self-Inflicted Violence*, the main difference between self-injury and tattoos and piercings is attitude. Alderman, a clinical psychologist, states that

most people who get tattooed and/or pierced are proud of their new decorations. They want to show others their ink, their studs, their plugs.

They want to tell the story of the pain, the fear, the experience. In contrast, those who hurt themselves generally don't tell anyone about it. Self-injurers go to great lengths to cover and disguise their wounds and scars. Self-injurers are not proud of their new decorations.[8]

Certainly, there are cases of people who deliberately and repeatedly pierce their bodies in an effort to reduce their emotional stress. However, if a person damages his or her body as part of a cultural ritual, or in order to increase attractiveness, or to pass through a certain rite of passage, then this is not considered SI.

Masochism

Some people take sexual pleasure from pain. Masochism is a psychiatric condition in which a person gets sexual gratification from being hurt, humiliated, or dominated by another person. To be considered a disorder, a person has to have experienced this type of sexual pleasure for at least six months, and it needs to cause significant problems in the person's work or family life. Self-injurers are not masochistic. First, they perform the injury to their bodies themselves rather than have other people do it; and second, self-injurers want relief from emotional suffering. They do not seek out pain for erotic pleasure.[9]

Suicide Attempt

While self-injury involves damage to the body without the intent to die, suicidal behaviors are specifically intended to end one's life. Hanging oneself, jumping off tall buildings, or slicing an artery all have death as their goal. Data drawn from community samples show that 4–8 percent of teenagers report having made at least one suicide attempt, and among institutional populations, this figure rises to 24–33 percent of youth. According to the World Health Organization, suicide is the fourth leading cause of death, worldwide, for people aged fifteen to forty-four.[10]

For a long time, the medical profession believed that people who self-injured were suicidal, but the behaviors differ in three important ways: the person's intent; the repetition of the act; and the degree of lethality of the injury.[11] People who self-injure do not intend to kill themselves, and they do not see death as a potential outcome of their actions. On the contrary, most people who self-harm believe it is a life-sustaining act, not a life-ending act. One sixteen-year-old girl said, "If I wanted to kill myself, I wouldn't burn stupid holes in my skin. I want to kill the pain, and that's the only thing that helps."[12] To someone who does not self-injure, this seems a paradox. Hurt yourself to stop hurting. But most studies find that people who self-injure are trying to avoid suicide.[13]

Additionally, people who self-injure harm themselves much more frequently and much less severely than those who engage in suicidal behavior. This is especially true for people in mental health facilities or hospitals. In one sample of inpatients, the average number of self-injury episodes over the course of a year was eighty as opposed to less than three suicide attempts.[14] While biting, burning, and cutting can lead to infection and scarring, they are much less likely to kill you than is an overdose or stringing a noose around your neck and kicking the chair out from under you. The low lethality of methods of SI go back to a person's intent: people who self-injure do not want to die; they want to live.

However, the relationship between suicide and self-injury is complicated. SI can be fatal. Sometimes the person simply cuts too deep, accidentally or while in a mental fog. But suicide attempts by self-injurers are not just a result of an accident. Some studies show that as many as 50 percent of people who die by suicide have a history of self-injury.[15] Research indicates that about 40 percent of people who self-injure think about suicide while they are harming themselves, and somewhere between 50 percent and 80 percent of people who self-injure have tried to commit suicide at least once. That statistic of 50–80 percent is a wide range and reveals how little is still understood about SI, but clearly a relationship between self-harm and suicide exists.

To address the gap in research about why SI and suicidal behavior both occur in some people, a team of Canadian scientists conducted an extensive analysis of the literature on self-injury. They reviewed thirty-one studies that either directly or indirectly looked for a link between suicidal behavior and SI. Consistently across all studies the researchers found that self-harm was a predictor of suicidal thoughts and behavior. However, the opposite was not true. Suicide attempts did not lead to episodes of self-injury later in life.[16]

The researchers also uncovered other variations in the relationship between SI and suicide. Several studies revealed that the more frequently a person self-injured, the more likely she was to attempt suicide. Additionally, while all forms of SI were predictive of suicidal thoughts, the more severe the method of self-injury, the greater the risk that the individual would attempt suicide. For example, one study found that people who engaged in moderate SI, such as hair pulling, were two times more likely to report a suicide attempt than someone who had never self-harmed. However, people who chose more severe forms of SI, including cutting and burning, reported suicide attempts at a rate ten times greater than people without self-injury disorder. The research also indicates that youth with histories of both SI and suicidal behavior are more likely to be depressed and impulsive, and they report greater incidence of family conflict and diagnoses of post-traumatic stress disorder.[17]

So why does one teen self-injure but never attempt suicide while another youth will make that leap from harm to death? There is no definitive answer, but three different theories offer alternative explanations. Self-injury and suicide lie on a continuum of destructive behavior. The *gateway theory* suggests that once a person deliberately hurts him- or herself, it is easier to slide down that continuum from a moderate injury to a lethal one. For example, if you become accustomed to cutting your forearm time after time, it is not such a great leap to move to slitting your wrist. An analogy that proponents of the gateway theory use is marijuana. Pot is a seemingly harmless drug in the eyes of many people. But experts on drug addiction maintain that marijuana is a gateway drug. It is often the first drug that addicts experiment with before moving on to more dangerous and addictive substances.[18] For the gateway theory to have scientific credibility, it requires more longitudinal research. We cannot know with any certainty if large numbers of self-injurers graduate from moderate harm to potentially lethal behavior until more studies are conducted that follow people from their teenage acts of self-injury into later life when they may or may not attempt suicide.

A second theory about the relationship between SI and suicide is called the *third variable theory*. Researchers who believe in this model argue that self-injury disorder and suicide are not directly connected. Rather, they are both caused by another condition. For example, 90 percent of people who die from suicide have a diagnosed psychiatric disorder, and about 87 percent of self-injuring youth from inpatient populations also have another diagnosis, such as borderline personality disorder. So proponents of the third variable theory argue that it is this

Celebrity Spotlight: Amy Winehouse

Amy Winehouse was an extremely talented British musician who self-destructed. Born in England, Winehouse released her debut album, *Frank*, when she was only twenty years old. Her single "Rehab" became a major hit, featuring what *Rolling Stone* magazine called her "brassy, sweet-and-sour voice." But rehab was exactly what Winehouse seemed unable to do.[b]

She battled drug and alcohol addictions, bulimia, self-harm, and destructive relationships. Even as she won five Grammy Awards in 2008, her fans and family waited for her to have another mental meltdown. Although Winehouse eventually kicked hard drugs, she continued to abuse alcohol, even appearing drunk at a concert. On July 23, 2011, at the age of twenty-seven, Amy Winehouse was found dead in her home as a result of alcohol poisoning.[c]

other mental illness that actually causes both the SI and suicidal behavior. Even if a self-injurer or a suicidal person is not diagnosed with a major mental illness, both groups do report high rates of depression, low self-esteem, and low levels of parental support. Apparently, people with SI and suicidal tendencies share common risk factors, which may account for the fact that people who self-injure also attempt, or at least consider, suicide. However, like the gateway theory, the third variable theory too needs to be more researched. It does not explain why so many people with significant rates of psychological disorders or childhood trauma attempt suicide but have no history of self-injury.[19]

A third theory that attempts to explain the relationship between self-injury and suicide is called Joiner's theory of acquired capability for suicide. The philosophy goes like this: Before a person will attempt suicide, he or she first must overcome the fear and pain associated with the behavior required to end one's life. Self-injury, over the course of time, desensitizes an individual to distress and discomfort and, therefore, makes one more capable of committing suicide. According to this theory, self-injury is not the only type of behavior that can steer one in the direction of suicide. Drug and alcohol abuse can have this effect, and so can exposure to violence. But another component to the theory of acquired capability is that the individual also needs to feel isolated and burdensome.[20] Evidence that supports Joiner's theory is that self-injurers who do attempt suicide have a long history of self-harm and use multiple methods to injure themselves.[21]

However, just like the other two theories, the acquired capability theory also has its critics. People who self-harm and those who attempt suicide usually use different methods. For example, just because a person becomes accustomed to the pain and fear associated with cutting, it does not logically follow that this person will not have any anxiety about taking a drug overdose—a very different experience. Also, some researchers argue that people who engage in both self-harm and suicidal behavior may just naturally have a higher pain tolerance than people who do not hurt themselves. Perhaps they do not need to become accustomed to fear and pain; they simply do not feel these things the way most people do.[22] While all three theories have their supporters and detractors, one point is clear: more research needs to be done on the connection between suicide and self-harm.

Despite the grim statistics that suggest that some people with SI will attempt suicide, other data shows that the majority of self-injurers, about 60 percent, report never having considered ending their lives.[23] One struggling teen described the motivation of most people who self-injure in an essay for the online magazine *Teen Ink*:

Contrary to popular belief, not all people who hurt themselves are suicidal. Quite the opposite—most people who self-injure are fighting to live. It's a coping mechanism; somehow, the pain keeps us sane and connected to

---

Teen Voice: "Self-Harm Does Lots of Harm"

One teen posted an essay on a website in which she voiced her frustration about the casual attitude some people have toward self-injury disorder. She was upset when she overheard another student joking and laughing about a student who had hurt herself: "She didn't kill herself, so it doesn't matter." This young writer knows that self-harm can be deadly. "People think that because individuals who self-harm don't always die from it, that it's not as big of an issue as attempting . . . suicide. Self-harm is number twenty-one on the list of ways to kill yourself."[d]

---

the world. After I cut, I felt numb, totally separate from everything that hurt me. I lived for that feeling, when the scarlet spread and the ache in my chest subsided.[24]

This teen's response is echoed by many self-injurers. They do not identify themselves as suicidal.[25] So perhaps the most accurate way to describe the relationship between SI and suicide is to say that self-harm is a sign of a person's emotional distress, and if these troubles are not successfully managed, they can lead to suicide.

Nature or Nurture

Self-preservation is a basic instinct. But how a person protects him- or herself is a learned behavior. As children, we try on new behaviors to see how they work, and then we either repeat them or quit doing them. Behaviors can be learned directly, such as a father who tells his children to say please every time they want something. Or behavior can be learned indirectly through inference. If you study for a history test and get an A, you conclude that studying helps you earn high marks. Thereafter, you study for every test.

Negative behaviors are learned too. This account of one anonymous teen's story demonstrates how self-injury can quickly become a habit: "I just got really, really upset, and I got into this mood . . . where I feel totally helpless with no end in sight. So, I went to my make-up bag, got my tweezers, and cut my arm. It didn't draw blood, but it left good marks. I never thought I'd do it again. . . . Soon enough I was making trips to the hardware store to buy blades that most people put in their utility knives."[26]

Some people might go for a run or eat a box of candy or smoke a joint when they feel stressed. But this teenager turned to her tweezers for relief. Why? Researchers who study the teenage brain find that they are programmed for experimentation and risk taking, even when the consequences are high. A 2010 study by Stephanie Burnett of University College London's Institute of Cognitive Neuroscience tested male risk-taking responses through computer games. Her study of a group of boys and men ages nine to thirty-five demonstrated that the male teenagers chose a risky option the most often and experienced the greatest thrill when they were put at risk. Jason Chein, a Temple University psychologist, stated that the part of the brain that processes emotional rewards changes rapidly in teenage years. In contrast, the executive part of the brain that exerts control over our impulses matures more slowly, often not reaching its full development until we are in our midtwenties.[27] So when the teenager quoted earlier reached for those tweezers, it is likely that her emotions propelled her, not the rational part of her brain.

Self-injury is a complicated mental disorder. There are psychological, neurological, and sociological factors that determine the type of coping mechanism a person chooses as a response to stress, and we will explore those complex causes in chapter 4. But it is important to understand that mental health professionals group people into different categories by their degrees and type of self-harm.

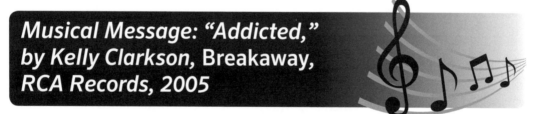

Musical Message: "Addicted," by Kelly Clarkson, Breakaway, RCA Records, 2005

The song "Addiction" by pop artist Kelly Clarkson is about being hooked. She does not specify if the addictive substance is a drug or a relationship or a behavior like self-harm. But that fact is irrelevant to the power of this music. The message of the song is intense: "It's like I can't breathe. It's like I can't see anything. Nothing but you. I'm addicted to you." Medical experts still debate whether self-injury is chemically addictive the way drugs and alcohol are. But there is no doubt that self-injurious behavior can become a crutch that some people have trouble living without.[e]

Categories of Self-Injurers

In the late 1980s, Dr. Armando Favazza was the first person to differentiate self-injurers into categories. He labeled these groups as major, stereotypic, compulsive, and impulsive. These classifications help mental health professionals determine what type of treatment may best help a person.

Major Self-Injury

According to Dr. Favazza, a person is a *major* self-harmer if his or her behavior is rare and extreme, such as sawing off a limb or plucking out an eye. In about 75 percent of these cases, the self-injurer suffers from a severe mental illness. He or she may have schizophrenia or may have suffered a temporary psychotic breakdown. Psychosis is a state in which people lose touch with reality. They have delusions and hallucinations and cannot distinguish between what is real and what they only imagine. They hear voices or smell or taste things that are only in their

People in a psychotic state lose touch with reality.

minds. Their thoughts are scattered and bizarre, and psychotics may have false beliefs that they are being persecuted or are famous.[28]

Some psychotics appear very nonchalant about their extreme mutilation of their bodies. The reasons for cutting of a hand, or castrating oneself, or gouging out one's own eyes seem rational to them at the time. Perhaps, they believe God commanded they hurt themselves or maybe they fear giving in to homosexual urges. The damage major self-injurers do to their bodies is a quick resolution to whatever inner crisis they were experiencing. However, that resolution is usually only temporary. Their self-harm soon returns with a vengeance.[29]

Stereotypic Self-Injury

The second category of self-harm is called stereotypic. This type of self-injury involves monotonous, repetitive acts—head banging, biting oneself, face and head slapping, pressing one's eyes. These acts often have a rhythmic pattern. Unlike other forms of self-harm, stereotypic injurers hurt themselves openly and in the presence of others. There does not appear to be any symbolism associated with the damage stereotypic injurers do to their bodies. Rather, it is biological need that drives them. These self-injurers are usually moderately or severely retarded or they have severe autism.[30]

Musical Message: "Bad Habit," by the Dresden Dolls, The Dresden Dolls, Roadrunner Records, 2004

The fast-paced, almost peppy, tune "Bad Habit" was featured on the debut album of Amanda Palmer and Brian Viglione, the punk duo known as the Dresden Dolls. The lyrics read like a clear-cut explanation for why a person would choose to self-injure: "When I open a familiar scar. Pain goes shooting like a star. Comfort hasn't failed to follow so far." The song goes on to argue that even if some people might say the habit of self-harm is self-indulgent, it is more productive than healthy behavior. Amanda Palmer said the lyrics were about her nail-biting habit. The repeated, compulsive biting of the finger nails and cuticles is one form of self-injury. It may sound innocent; however, nail biters nibble and gnaw at their fingers so obsessively that the skin rips away and wounds do not have a chance to heal.[f]

Compulsive Self-Injury

Many people bite their nails, a childhood habit we often outgrow. But compulsive self-injurers may bite their nails or scratch their skin or pull out their hair, repetitively and severely, as a tool to manage anxiety.[31] This type of self-harm falls within the category of obsessive-compulsive disorder, a defined mental illness.

One twenty-five-year-old man Dr. Favazza encountered scratched his entire body, except for his genitals and back, completely raw. This condition is called psychogenic skin excoriation. It involves the repetitive and extreme rubbing, scratching, and picking at one's skin. Often people who do this are anxious and depressed.[32]

Hair pulling, or trichotillomania, is another obsessive-compulsive disorder. People who suffer from this condition pluck their eyebrows, eyelashes, scalp hair, and even their pubic hair, often automatically, without awareness. But other times the person will pluck her or his hair to avoid other troubling thoughts or urges. People with trichotillomania also are often anxious and depressed.[33]

Humans are not the only animals to damage the bodies in an effort to soothe themselves. A stressed-out cat can lick itself to the bone with its sandpaper tongue. The official diagnosis of this behavior is psychogenic alopecia, but "closet lickers" is the layman's terms for cats that lick themselves until their fur falls out and red sores break out on their skin. It is a stress-relieving behavior. Some dog

Movie Review: Winter Passing, Directed by Darrell Larson, Twentieth Century Fox, 2005

Reese Holden is a troubled, young actress trying to make it in New York City. The daughter of two famous authors, Reese has severed ties with her parents, not even returning home for her mother's funeral. She manages feelings of alienation and depression with casual sex, alcohol, and drugs, and by slamming her hand inside a drawer when feelings become too much.

When an editor offers Reese a small fortune to publish the letters Reese's father wrote to her mother when they were young, Reese heads home. There she finds a would-be musician and a graduate student keeping house with Reese's dad. As she vies with these two houseguests for her father's attention, Reese gradually comes to terms with her own past.

breeds, including Labradors and golden retrievers, obsessively gnaw and lick at a limb or the base of the tail. Horses might nip at their own flanks or spontaneously and violently buck and spin and kick. Vets call pets that circle furniture for hours or rub their gums on furniture until it bleeds "stereotypies."[34] This label is similar to the label Dr. Armando Favazza used to label severely retarded people who self-injure.

Impulsive Self-Injury

The fourth category of self-injury is the one that is the focus of this book—impulsive self-injury. This form of self-harm is the most common. These are people who cut, bite, pull hair, or carve their skin. They may do it compulsively and frequently or just on occasion. Dr. Favazza labeled this category impulsive because a person experiences an impulse or desire to self-harm that he cannot resist. Once the act of injury is complete, about two-thirds of people feel immediate relief and one-third of those still feel better several hours later, some even days later.[35]

There is a difference between episodic self-injurers and repetitive ones. Some people may self-harm on occasion when the stress of life overwhelms them while others become preoccupied with the desire to harm themselves. Self-injury becomes part of how they identify themselves. *I am a cutter. I am a burner.* The injurious behavior of repetitive harmers seems to be on autopilot rather than in reaction to any crisis in life. These people may describe themselves as addicted to self-harm. There is no magic number at which point an episodic self-injurer becomes a repetitive one.[36] The change begins internally when the person starts to obsess over the act of injury, and then the behavior increases in frequency and severity.

The Woman Who Ate Cutlery

Although Dr. Favazza's categories of self-injury can be helpful in treating patients, not everyone fits neatly into his defined groups. Take the bizarre case of the woman who ate cutlery. She has been hospitalized at least seventy-two times. She has swallowed dozens of forks and spoons and batteries, and she inserted sharp objects or large doses of medication into her vagina. However, she is not psychotic. She knows what she has done, who she is, and where she is. Each time she self-injures, she goes to the emergency room for treatment. The example of the woman who ate cutlery reveals just how complicated the human brain is.[9]

Methods and Frequency of Self-Harm

People inflict pain on their bodies in multiple ways and with different degrees of frequency (table 3.1 shows some common methods). About 8–10 percent of the three million or so Americans who self-injure do so chronically, which means with regularity.[37] A 2008 study reported in the *Journal of Clinical Child Adolescent Psychology* found that 23 percent of people who self-injured did so between eleven and fifty times; and almost 10 percent of people reported harming themselves more than fifty times.[38] Seventy-five percent of these people use multiple methods to damage their bodies, a conclusion that has been reached by several other studies as well.[39]

In 2006, Janis Whitlock, the director of the Cornell Research Program on Self-Injurious Behavior in Adolescence and Young Adults, randomly sampled

Table 3.1 Common Self-Injury Methods

Method of Self-Injury	Average Percent of Self-Injurers Who Use This Method
Cutting	71%
Burning	27%
Self-hitting	35%
Interference with wound healing	22%
Inserting objects	22%
Picking skin	11.1%
Hair pulling	10%
Bone breaking	8%
Multiple methods	78%

Sources: Patricia Adler and Peter Adler, *Tender Cut: Inside the Hidden World of Self-Injury* (New York: New York University Press, 2011); Andrea L. Barrocas et al., "Rates of Nonsuicidal Self-Injury in Youth: Age, Sex, and Behavioral Methods in a Community Sample," *Pediatrics* 130, no. 1 (2012): 39–45, http://www.ncbi.nlm.nih.gov/pmc/articles/PMC3382916/.

students from eight universities. Almost twelve thousand students responded to the study's survey, and of these, 15.3 percent reported a history of self-injury and 6.8 percent had harmed themselves in the last year. Almost 85 percent of the students who reported self-injury had done it more than once, and almost half reported harming themselves more than six times.[40] Researchers were able to gain data about the methods young adults use to harm themselves from the information they shared on their surveys.

More than half of the students reported that they severely scratched or pinched their skin, either with their fingers or other objects, until it bled and bruised. Obsessive picking at skin can be a disorder known as dermotillomania, a type of obsessive compulsive disorder that is somewhat different than SI.[41]

Cutting, which has become a word synonymous with self-injury, was practiced by about one-third of the college students.[42] Some cutters might scratch spider-

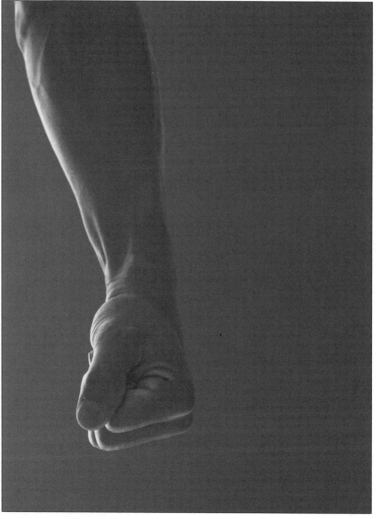

Some people punch or kick walls in order to break their own bones.

web lines in their skin or just nick the skin whereas others must gouge. Vanessa began to self-injure as a college freshman. She started by using a sharp piece of plastic to make small scratches on her skin. When that no longer gave her release, she transitioned to razor blades and knives.[43] Some self-injurers stick to the same tools, but increase the frequency of their acts. One teen named Kris described how she began with a light scratch on her arm maybe once a week. Then she began cutting two to three times a week, and then four to five times a day.[44]

Cutting is only one in the long list of methods people use to hurt themselves. In the 2006 study, many college students reported ripping their skin, carving letters into their skin, inserting sharp objects like pins and glass into their skin, punching themselves with closed fists, banging their heads into walls, pulling their hair out, and picking at their scabs so their wounds could never heal.[45]

Burning was also cited by about 13 percent of the college students.[46] People are innovative in the tools they use to burn themselves. Matches, lighters, grill igniters, chemicals, and stove tops. Adam was a young man who shifted from cutting to burning. When Adam was a child, his stepfather had beaten him with a belt. As he grew older, and life became more stressful, Adam said, "I was trying to get ready for college, and I would just have more issues to deal with in life. . . . So

Read about It: Sharp (New York: HarperCollins, 2012)

Sharp is the gripping memoir of David Fitzpatrick's almost twenty-year struggle with self-injury. He suffers from bipolar disorder, a mental illness characterized by alternating bouts of deep depression and extreme mania. The first time Fitzpatrick cut himself was after his girlfriend broke up with him. He read her breakup letter out loud and cut seven slices into his forearm. Fitzpatrick said the sensation comforted him the way milk and cookies did when he was young. He was hooked.

Fitzpatrick's self-injury was extreme and this memoir is graphic and painful to read. Fitzpatrick burned himself and cut himself, even slicing off pieces of his own fingers and ears. From age twenty to forty-one, he was in and out of mental health facilities. Self-injury was how he coped with anxiety, depression, and self-loathing. But *Sharp* is also a story of recovery—hard-earned, but hopeful. One reads it and thinks that if David Fitzpatrick can recover from self-injury, everyone can.[h]

I decided to try something new."[47] He began to burn himself. "And I think doing that was definitely more intense because there's sounds and smells and stuff, and it's a lot more of an intense way to deal with the issue."[48] And intensity is what self-injurers seek.

Erica was a college student who had been abused for years by her older brother. She started self-injuring when she was twelve by scratching herself with her fingernails. Eventually she used an X-Acto knife instead, and by her sophomore year she had discovered burning. She would hold her curling iron to her skin until a large blister formed. For Erica the burns were far worse than the cuts. "I—like, obviously it doesn't hurt when you're doing it but afterward. No one's going to tell me that theirs don't hurt. There's no way in hell. That you don't wake up in the middle of the night and just not be able to move. The burns were so much worse after . . . the tightness. . . . So I didn't burn that much because of that. But I liked it."[49] No matter the method used, the injury brings release, and this is what the person wants more than anything else in the moment she picks up the tool to hurt herself.

About three-quarters of self-injurers use more than one method to harm themselves. This switching from one method to another might be due to a variety of factors. The self-injurer might be transferred to a hospital or treatment center where his injury options are limited. He may become tolerant to a certain kind of injury and seek a more intense sensation.[50] Or the type of method a person chooses may just be a matter of personal choice.

One eighteen-year-old premed student chose a method that matched her mood. When she was sad, she cut herself. When she was angry, she burned her skin.[51] Self-injurers are inventive. They may break their bones, chew their lips, gnaw on their tongues, or strip off hangnails with their teeth. They may embed sharp objects like the woman who inserted fishhooks into her vagina. Another woman cut and burned herself and then smeared her own feces into these wounds

---

Teen Voice: Poetry

Self-injurers reveal their inner emotions on the outside of their bodies. Poetry is a powerful way to communicate deep feelings through imagery and rhyme. This is an excerpt of how one young poet expressed her feelings on the e-zine *Teen Ink*. "Love carved into flesh . . ./Burning relief/Anger carved into skin . . ./ The sharp pain stops/Healing begins/Tears still come down/Waiting for the cycle to repeat again."[i]

in order to infect them.[52] However, these are extreme cases that came to the attention of medical professionals. Most self-injurers wound themselves privately and quietly on hidden places on their body. They may never come to the attention of doctors or psychiatrists. It is these people who make up the bulk of the silent, suffering self-injurers.

Just like some people have a preferred method of self-injury, many also have a preferred spot on the body (see table 3.2). Usually this location has to do with pain and secrecy. According to a 2008 study in the *Journal of Advanced Nursing*, the most common areas for people to injure are the wrists, arms, ankles, calves, inner thighs, belly, bra line, panty line, armpits, and feet.[53] Informal and anecdotal data reveals that people injure themselves in areas that are easiest to hide. The

Table 3.2 Preferred Areas on Body to Injure

Area on Body	Percentage
Forearms	33%
Upper legs	30%
Stomach	8%
Upper arms	6%
Lower legs	6%
Feet	2%
Other	6%
Chest	2%
Internal (overdosing)	1%
Hands	1%

Sources: "Where on Your Body Do You Most Harm Yourself?" Self-Injury.net, March 26, 2014, https://self-injury.net/self-injurers/polls/where-your-body-do-you-most-often-harm-yourself (accessed December 31, 2014).

Answers and Assistance

The Adolescent Self-Injury Foundation is a nonprofit group dedicated to raising awareness and understanding of self-injury. The group was founded in 2010 by Joann Goodman, a licensed social worker who has spent decades working with teenagers and young adults who self-injure. This foundation provides educational resources for caregivers on the newest and most effective treatments for self-injury disorder. The website, SelfInjuryFoundation.org, provides helpful links for self-injurers including "146 Things You Can Do Besides Self-Harm." Goodman has incorporated animal therapy into her practice. Panda and Cosmos, two of her dogs, are featured on the website.[j]

website Self-Injury.net conducted a poll of 847 viewers. They were asked where on their body they most often harmed. One participant in the poll said that she cut herself anywhere she could hide it. She would cut on her shoulders until the weather turned warm. When she wanted to wear tank tops, she would instead wound her stomach. She said that she "needed to see what the hurt I was feeling looked like."[54] Finding a new and satisfying location to harm is a continuing challenge for chronic injurers. One twenty-two-year-old named Jessie even cut the bottoms of her feet. This gave her the additional benefit of being able to push her foot into the ground to cause herself pain if she was not able to cut herself in a particularly stressful moment.[55]

Wrap-Up

Now you know how self-injury differs from other tissue-damaging procedures we do to our bodies. You have learned that there are four main types of self-injurers and that impulsive self-injury is the most common. And we have examined how, where on the body, and how often people harm themselves. The most complicated and mysterious part of self-injury disorder is why people do it. That is the topic of the next chapter.

4

CUTTING OUT
THE PAIN

....

These are the best years of your life. Has an adult ever said that to you? Young people do not have the responsibilities of a career ladder to climb, a family to support, or a mortgage to pay. Therefore, adults often look back on their high school and college years with nostalgia. Such freedom. Such fun.

Reality is not such a pretty picture. Adolescence and young adulthood can be the most difficult years of our lives. Not coincidentally, this is the time when most people begin to self-injure.

During the years from puberty through the early twenties, you face some critical psychological tasks. You are forming your identity. You are testing out independence. Your responsibilities have increased. At the same time, your body is changing and your emotions ricochet from happy to sad fast enough to give you whiplash.

Life confronts you with difficult choices, and it is hard to know what path is the right one. For example, what if you have always been a straight A student? Then you meet a guy you really like. He wants you to cut class and go to the beach with him. What do you do? Play it safe and follow the rules or take a risk that might get you in trouble?

You pick the beach and the boy.

The school administration busts you. Your parents find out and ground you. You are stuck in your bedroom, lonely and isolated and angry. The whirlpool of emotions that churns in your brain makes it hard to think. You have to do something to clear your head.

This kind of internal struggle forges our identity. While our sense of self is shaped throughout life, it is a vital developmental task of our teenage and young adult years. Confusion over identity, even in well-adjusted teens, can lead to depression, anxiety, and anger. Some youth ride through these years with relative ease and manage their emotions in healthy ways. But many young people attempt to escape their stress through dangerous coping mechanisms. Some abuse drugs and alcohol. Some develop eating disorders. Still others self-injure. What types of people choose self-injury over other coping mechanisms and the reasons why they choose to do so are the subjects of this chapter.

Identity formation is the key developmental task of adolescence and young adulthood.

Equal Opportunity Disorder

Race and Ethnicity

For a long time, mental health experts believed that the typical self-injurer was a white, middle-class female who had above average intelligence.[1] This view has changed. People of all racial and ethnic groups self-injure. A 2012 study by the University of Mississippi Medical Center found that African American middle school boys were the group most likely to self-injure, followed by white female teens.[2] Dr. Kim Gratz, the psychologist who conducted the study, said, "Often times when people think of cutting or other self-harm, they imagine a white girl. No one thinks of an African-American boy."[3] Out of the 1,931 students Gratz surveyed in grades 6 through 12, African American middle school youth reported higher rates of self-harm than their same age, white peers. By high school, whites had higher rates than blacks. The scope and findings of this study are significant because it is the first study to survey enough African American youth to obtain a statistically significant sample.[4]

More research needs to be done to determine the degree to which nonwhite teenagers and young adults harm themselves. The few studies that have examined their results for racial and ethnic data are contradictory. Some found that African American and Hispanic college students were as likely to self-injure as their white peers, while other studies found that black, Hispanic, and Asian students were less likely to injure than were the white students. But the number of nonwhites included in these studies was small, less than one-third of the total respondents.[5]

In 2013, a group of researchers attempted to remedy this gap in research. They drew names from the 2005 to 2009 archives of a public college in New York City and contacted students who had formerly been in undergraduate psychology classes. The students who agreed to be interviewed completed a survey. Of those who responded, 62 percent were female, 50 percent identified as Hispanic, 28 percent as black, 16 percent as white, and 6 percent as Asian.[6] The results showed that 26 percent of these young adults reported clinical self-injury. That means that they had deliberately harmed themselves at least five times in their lives. The white and Asian respondents had a one in five rate of self-injury, while blacks and Hispanics shared a rate that was one out of ten (see table 4.1).[7]

Table 4.1 Self-Injury Rates among Minority Populations

Minority Group	Black	Hispanic	White	Asian	Sexual Minority Youth
Percent who reported at least five instances of self-injuring	9.2%	10.4%	21.4%	21.7%	72.5
Total number of responders in the study	196	356	115	42	95

Sources: Megan S. Chesin, Aviva N. Moster, and Elizabeth L. Jeglic, "Non-Suicidal Self-Injury Among Ethnically and Racially Diverse Emerging Adults: Do Factors Unique to the Minority Experience Matter?" *Current Psychology* 32, no. 4 (2013): 318–328, Academic Search Premier, EBSCOhost; Sarah J. Nickels et al., "Differences in Motivations of Cutting Behavior among Sexual Minority Youth." *Child & Adolescent Social Work Journal* 29, no. 1 (2012): 41–59, Academic Search Premier, EBSCOhost.

Before conducting this study, the researchers had hypothesized that perceived or actual racism or a lack of identification with their racial or ethnic group would result in higher rates of self-injury among nonwhite students. However, the results did not support this position. The only variables that influenced whether a student was more likely to report greater incidences of self-harm was a diagnosis of either bipolar disorder or anxiety.[8]

The results of both the New York and the Mississippi studies reveal that self-injury is not just a white girl's disorder, and more research needs to be done before we can fully understand the experience of self-injury for nonwhite youth.

Sexual Orientation

The term *sexual minority* refers to people who identify as lesbian, gay, bisexual, transgender, or queer (LGBTQ). Self-injury affects youth from these minorities; however, the data on these groups is limited and complicated. A 2009 study of high school students in Massachusetts revealed a gender difference among students who cut themselves. Only 14.3 percent of females in a sexual minority reported cutting as opposed to 41.7 percent of sexual minority males. However, a 2010 study concluded that lesbian and bisexual females reported higher rates of cutting than did gay and bisexual males. The reason for these contradictory results is not clear.[9]

Other conclusions are consistent from numerous studies. Transgender youth are at the highest risk for self-injury. The data also indicates that the rates of self-injury among populations of sexual minorities vary depending on other factors. Homelessness, physical abuse, bullying, depression, and anxiety are all issues that increase the likelihood of self-injury in straight youth and have the same effect on teens from a sexual minority. Studies have also found that the earlier in life a young person reveals his or her sexual identity, the greater the risk of engaging in self-harm.[10]

On the surface, this might seem illogical. If young persons are confident enough to tell people that they are gay, you would assume they have a strong sense of identity. However, revealing your sexual identity at a young age also means you have more years in which to be bullied and discriminated against. This happened to one teen who posted her story on *Teen Ink*. From childhood she knew she was different from her playmates. "I always knew I was different. I felt out of place, like I didn't really belong, didn't really fit in, but I never could figure out what it was that made me different."[11] She was the tomboy, the tough kid, the funny one. But inside she hurt. Then in the fifth grade this teen experienced her first crush on a girl. "At first I denied, denied, denied. There was no way I could be bisexual or a lesbian, I told myself. Imagine trying to explain that to my friends and family,

I thought. In fifth grade when words like gay and faggot are often synonymous to stupid and dumb, there was no way I wanted to face those realities."[12]

So this girl decided to call herself bisexual. And a year later, at two o'clock in the morning during a sleepover, she told her twelve-year-old best friend that she thought she might be bisexual. Her friend's response: "Cool." This welcome reaction convinced the teen to come out to other people. But not everyone was as tolerant as the girl's friend. One boy, in particular, intimidated her. "Bull Dyke," he would say if he ran into her in the hallway. The teen recalled, "I . . . always pretended that words couldn't get the best of me, but those words did get the best of me, in that situation. Those words hurt. More than sticks and stones. In fact they hurt so much, that I started cutting myself."[13] Being seen as different from your peers is difficult at any age. For a middle school lesbian girl, it can be devastating.

Gender

A common misperception is that self-injury disorder only affects females. This is inaccurate, but the degree to which males self-injure is still a matter of debate. Some studies report that the disorder is equally divided between males and females; others have found that females are four times more likely to self-injure than males.[14] There may be two reasons for the gap in these results. One reason is that in general males are less willing to report self-injury. They are trained to cover up any signs of weakness. One guy told his therapist that he never told anyone that he was a cutter because his friends would think it was "really gay."[15] A second reason is that some studies include suicidal behavior as part of their analysis and that alters the data.[16]

In an effort to narrow the knowledge gap about gender and self-injury, Janis Whitlock, a research scientist in the Bronfenbrenner Center for Translational Research and the director of the Cornell Research Program on Self-Injury and Recovery, conducted a massive study in 2006 and 2007. Whitlock and her team of researchers randomly sampled 14,372 college students from eight Midwest schools. Information was solicited from the students through a web-based wellness survey. The results show that there is a gender difference in the rates of self-injury. Females in the study reported self-injuring at a rate almost twice that of males: 18.9 percent compared to 10.9 percent. Females also reported a greater number of incidences of self-injury over the course of their lives. However, males reported as many incidences of self-injury as females in the past year. College is a stressful time of life for both genders.[17]

Males and females do use different methods of self-injury. While females are more likely to scratch and cut, guys tend to punch objects or people or themselves.[18]

Females report that they wound their arms, wrists, and thighs. For guys, the hands are the primary target. The researchers concluded that the location of injury might help explain why self-injury is seen as a female disorder.[19] Thin scars on the arm conjure up an image of a girl slicing her arm with a razor blade. Banged up knuckles make a guy look like he has been in a fight, and that is a more socially acceptable response for a male.

Jimmy was one of the males that the Adlers interviewed for their book *The Tender Cut*. He described the masculine stereotype that pushes boys to fit into a certain role. "I play hockey, and I play drums. And I mean, hockey player. I mean, supposed to be an idiot brute."[20] Self-injury does not fit into this tough-guy image, unless, of course, your wound is harsh and you flaunt it. Which many males do.

Another young man the Adlers interviewed, James, described his observations of the wounds that guys and girls self-inflicted. "Guys I've known have cut deeper and left bigger scars. The ones they made . . . were very big and thick. The girls' scars . . . have been way more delicate."[21] Both Whitlock and the Adlers found that males self-injure in a social setting, often in fits of anger or while under the influence of drugs and alcohol. Young men, sometimes athletes or other masculine subgroups, engaged in acts like self-burning to prove their toughness and solidify their group identity. The Adlers interviewed a twenty-two-year-old man named Jason. He recalled how at age nine, he and a group of friends inserted mechanical pencils into electric sockets and held hands so the electric shock would travel from one guy to the next. The boys took turns sitting closest to the wall as that was where the shock was greatest. When these boys grew older, they moved on to group branding in which they heated up things like bottle caps and held them over their skin. However, Jason's description of these acts was not just a recollection of a group of immature boys seeking a thrill. "If we felt like we needed a pick-me-up, we would self-inflict ourselves. You know, sometimes you have to yell out and let all the emotions out, and I think that's what part of it was when it got to the part where we branded ourselves. It would be a long day, or you were mad at your parents. I can recall a couple instances where you would be mad at a bad athletic event. So heat up some metal and put a little mark on your body."[22]

Release—that was what Jason and his friends were looking for. That is what SI is all about. Self-harm is not just a "girl thing." Guys do it too. Reading stories about males who self-harm can help guys who struggle with this disorder realize that they are not alone.

Institutionalized Populations

For most people self-injury is a very private, secret act. However, there is anecdotal evidence that suggests the disorder can spread like a contagion among youth

Celebrity Spotlight: Russell Brand

Today Russell Brand is an international star, a comedian whose outrageous antics both offend and attract. But Brand's stardom was on shaky ground for a long time, especially in the years in which he struggled with addictions to drugs, sex, and self-injury. In one memorable incident, Brand showed up for his job as an MTV presenter dressed like Osama Bin Laden, the mastermind of the September 11, 2001, terrorist attacks that killed almost three thousand people. The date of Brand's appearance was September 12, 2001. The nation was still in shock and no one thought Brand's joke was funny. He was fired.

In his 2009 memoir, *My Booky Wook: A Memoir of Sex, Drugs, and Stand-Up,* Brand tells the story of how he began to self-injure at age thirteen or fourteen. Whenever he felt trapped or frustrated, he would slash himself with a knife or glass. This pattern continued well into his twenties. Once, Brand performed at a party at the drama school he attended. As Brand began to perform his mono- logue, everyone kept laughing and chatting with friends. He became irritated that people were not paying enough attention to what he was convinced was his *masterful performance.* So he drained a glass of vodka, smashed it on his head, and stabbed his chest with the broken glass and raked the sharp edge up and down his arms. The audience paid attention to that. They began to scream, and one student commented that while the party had been fun, he did not want to be an actor any longer. Brand's wry conclusion was that he had misjudged his audience.

Brand finally received treatment for drug, alcohol, and sex addiction, and he was eventually diagnosed with bipolar disorder. His self-injury was a complex symptom of his mental illness and other addictions.[a]

in schools, residential treatment centers, and juvenile detention centers. Many of these kids had emotional and behavior problems before being institutionalized. Once they are housed in close quarters in a setting where they have little control, if one person self-injures, others imitate the behavior.[23]

The Cornell Research Program on Self-Injury and Recovery suggests this epi- demic nature of SI is caused by groups of teens injuring as part of group mem- bership. They also cite the Internet and the coverage of SI in the media, which serves, in a perverse way, to educate youth that self-harm is an activity that some stressed out people use.[24]

A 2014 study of thousands of inmates of the New York City jail system revealed that those who received solitary confinement for breaking the rules were more likely to self-injure. Some inmates admitted that they hurt themselves to avoid solitary confinement. If they self-injured, corrections officers often worried that the inmates were suicidal and put them in a therapeutic setting instead of in *bing*—the slang term for solitary. The security staff called these inmates bing beaters.[25]

Males might be driven to their first act of self-injury when they are incarcerated because they have few other choices for external stimulation. Some men were possibly driven by thrill-seeking, risk-taking action, and that may be what got them into prison in the first place; now their movements are restricted. They cannot get into fights to release emotion, so they self-injure.[26]

Prisoners have little control over their lives. They are told when to wake up, when to exercise, when and what to eat, and when the lights go out. They cannot influence the world around them, but they can control what they do to their bodies. For some incarcerated people, self-injury is one method of exercising control over the system that holds them captive.[27]

As with other minority groups who self-injure, the prison population is understudied for a variety of reasons. The setting is a difficult one for researchers to access. The inmates may not be willing to volunteer information, and only the most serious cases are recorded by guards; therefore, the incidences of self-injury are probably underreported. However, there is another highly regimented institution—the military—where SI is also being studied.

Since 2003, the United States has been involved in active military conflicts in Iraq and Afghanistan. Life on and around the battlefield is one of the greatest stressors a person can experience. In the last decade the number of suicides and attempted suicides by members of the armed forces has doubled.[28] Because of the connection between SI and suicide, a 2014 study examined military veterans enrolled in college courses, trying to gauge to what extent they harmed themselves. Out of 355 survey respondents, the researchers found a lifetime self-injury rate of 14 percent. Cutting or carving the skin was the most common method of self-harm. This is important data. The rate of SI reported in this survey was much higher than a previous study done within the military that found that only 4 percent of veterans self-harmed. It is unclear whether that research was flawed or if the rates of SI are rising so dramatically.[29]

Two other aspects of the 2014 study are revealing: female student veterans were twice as likely to report self-injury as were the males, and almost half of the Native American respondents reported harming themselves. Interestingly, respondents who had served on combat support missions were twice as likely to report having self-harmed as those who had actually been in combat. This area needs further study, but one hypothesis is that the role of combat support has greater stressors than the military currently understands.[30]

Victims of Abuse or Trauma

While self-injurers come from all walks of life, one common factor shared by many is a history of trauma. Most studies of chronic self-injurers reveal that somewhere between 50 percent and 90 percent of them were sexually abused as children.[31] There is also a strong correlation between physical abuse as a child and cutting as a teenager.[32] In *A Bright Red Scream*, author Marilee Strong calls sexual abuse of a child "terrorism of the highest order."[33] The combination of fear, pain, and excitement on an immature brain is too intense. If the abuser is a trusted family member, then the damage is greater. The child may like the special attention she is receiving, but at the same time, she knows on some level that rape is a violation. The two emotions cannot be reconciled. Sexual abuse violates basic boundaries. As Wendy Lader, cofounder of the organization S.A.F.E. Alternatives, says, "The one thing that is really ours and that we have boundaries on is our body. When we talk about sexual abuse that is debilitating, we don't mean a woman who was raped when she was twenty years old. We're talking about a child who was abused by someone who was known, someone who is a caretaker. That results in very conflicted feelings about who you are, who another is, what's okay, what's not okay."[34]

Sometimes the situation is made worse when one guardian is the abuser and the other seems to be a silent partner. This was the case for Jackie. She was sexually abused by her stepfather, but when she told her mother, the woman refused to believe it. She sent Jackie across the country to live with her sister. Jackie had to raise her own money to return home and only after she promised to never bring up the abuse again.[35]

The Mentally Ill

Mental illness is another common feature of people who deliberately harm their bodies. For a long time, patients who sought help for self-injury were diagnosed with borderline personality disorder (BPD). Self-mutilation is one of the distinctive traits of this mental illness along with poor self-image, impulsivity, unstable relationships, intense anger, and paranoia.[36] Kiera Van Gelder wrote about what it was like to finally have a doctor verbally diagnosis her as having BPD. For years Kiera had felt empty. She attempted suicide. She cut herself. She could not maintain relationships or a job. Although she had seen psychiatrists and psychologists and therapists since age twelve, it was not until she was thirty-one that someone finally spelled out the problem that had ailed her most of her life—borderline personality disorder. Mental health experts consider patients with BPD the most difficult of all to treat, and consequently resist diagnosing them because of the stigma this label carries. However, the disorder is treatable, and as Kiera Van Gelder is learning, accepting the diagnosis is the first step to regaining control of one's life.[37]

However, BPD is not the only mental illness associated with SI. Mental health experts now understand that SI can appear alongside of several different mental illnesses. These include bipolar disorder, depression, anxiety, eating disorders, and schizophrenia. Additionally, to further complicate diagnosis and treatment, doctors are not always able to pinpoint the source of a person's troubles.[38]

Chloe defied all medical diagnosis. For most of her life, she has heard noises in her head—like a radio turned on low. But on bad days, the radio is cranked up. The voices are loud and critical. Chloe gave each voice a color—yellow was the meanest voice of all. It was noisy and rude. At around the age of seven or eight, Chloe began to disassociate, to disappear in her mind. She grew up believing she was crazy.[39]

Chloe was the good kid in the family. Her sister made frequent, dramatic scenes, but Chloe taught herself how to calm down quickly since that was what was expected of her. At the age of nine she cut herself with a knife. Her disassociation worsened. Once she lost two days, her only recollection of the vanished time a photograph of a reflection in a window pane—of herself, holding a gun. As the voices grew louder, cutting brought Chloe back to herself. "When the blade cut the surface and I saw blood, it would bring everything back into focus. But it didn't work for very long so I'd have to do it over and over again."[40]

Psychiatrist after psychiatrist; test after test; one medication after another. Chloe tried them all. Finally, the doctors performed a brain scan and found two

Teen Voices: "Ordinary Girl"

In recent years mental health professionals have recognized that many teenagers without a background characterized by severe trauma or mental illness still turn to self-harm as a way to cope with life's stress. One girl who posted on the e-zine *Teen Ink* already knew this fact. She reminded her readers that people who self-injure are not freaks. Many are not victims of rape or other abuse. "We are normal people who lead normal lives but we just don't exactly know how to cope with whatever is going on at the time. . . . We need to feel the pain, see the blood, cry the healing tears. It seems like it's the only thing that will help because nothing else does."[b]

cysts in her brain that had been causing seizures that showed up as noise. Chloe was put on an antiseizure medicine that finally stilled the voices.[41] But after all the years of struggle, cutting had become her survival mechanism, and it would not let go of her that quickly.

Eating Disorders

Researchers long suspected there was a link between eating disorders and self-injury. This connection was documented in 2010 when researchers from Stanford University School of Medicine and the Lucile Packard Children's Hospital examined records for almost 1,500 patients at an eating disorder clinic. These patients were mostly white females between the ages of ten and twenty-one. They discovered that 41 percent of the teen and young adults reported that they hurt themselves. This relationship is not surprising. Anorexia, bulimia, and self-injury are all maladaptive methods of reducing anxiety.[42]

Musical Message: "Ana's Song (Open Fire)" by Silverchair, Neon Ballroom, Murmur Records, 1999

The eating disorders anorexia and bulimia are forms of self-harm. While these disorders affect females in greater numbers, males are not immune. Daniel Johns, singer and songwriter of the band Silverchair, struggled with anorexia in the late 1990s. After his band became an almost overnight success, Johns grew increasingly anxious and paranoid. He retreated inside his house, hardly seeing anyone for a year and growing thinner and thinner each day. At the worst point, Johns was eating a couple of pieces of fruit a day and only weighed 110 pounds. His disorder was not about self-image; it was about control. "It was never about my body . . . I guess, I felt that my life was out of control and it was kind of out of my hands, I couldn't do anything about it, I guess I took control of food intake, because it was the only thing that no one could really take charge of." Johns' battle with anorexia is the subject of "Ana's Song." Ana is another name for anorexia. Johns pleads "Please die Ana . . . I need you somehow . . . I love you to the bones." Medication and writing poetry helped Johns heal.[c]

Fiona's story reveals the interplay of eating disorders and self-injury. She became anorexic at age sixteen. When her parents forced her to eat, she became bulimic. From age eighteen until twenty-three, she cut herself almost daily. For Fiona all three compulsions were driven by voices. Fiona was not schizophrenic. She knew the voices were not real, but they sent her messages just the same. *You're ugly. You're fat. Get the poison out. You'll feel better when you do.*[43]

One day Fiona realized she was dying. She only weighed seventy-six pounds and could barely breathe. She made her way to a cardiologist's office, and began a slow, excruciatingly slow road to recovery.[44]

Now you know something about the type of people who self-injure. They can be black or white, male or female, gay or straight, institutionalized or free, fat or thin, mentally ill or not. If that description seems to include everybody, that is because it does. The more researchers learn about SI, the more they realize how widespread this disorder is. In order to understand the strong hold SI has on its victims, we have to explore why they self-harm.

Why Self-Injure?

For most people, the very idea of self-injury is incomprehensible. We try to avoid pain, not seek it out. Pain is the body's way of telling you, *Hey, quit that. It hurts.* Therefore, if a person continues to do something that causes pain, he or she must be very motivated to either endure the hurt or ignore it. Self-injurers are driven by the most powerful of all motives—the will to survive.

If someone you loved was trapped in a burning building, would you rush in and try to save the person? I believe I would. Those who self-injure are desperately trying to rescue someone too—themselves.

As explained in chapter 1, people who self-injure do so because it relieves their emotional pain. But there are other ways to feel better. Some teens lift weights or go on a good crying jag or have a rip-roaring argument with the person who has made them angry. What is it that makes some people pick up a razor blade or a hammer to dull their inner pain?

While the causes of self-injury disorder are complex, they tend to fall into two distinct categories: psychology and biology.

Psychological Causes

Personality Traits

Most research suggests that we are born with certain personality types. Experts debate how many categories of character exist and how much our temperament evolves throughout life. However, psychologists recognize that people who self-injure have common personality traits. They tend to be impulsive and have trouble delaying gratification. These individuals feel compelled to eliminate their negative emotions immediately rather than riding them out until they dissipate on their own.

Self-injurers also feel negative emotions strongly. Sierra, my former student who self-injured, felt small slights intensely. During an activity, one of Sierra's friends decided to partner with another student. Sierra put her head down on the desk, convinced that both girls hated her. In seconds she had concluded that she was now friendless; that there must be something repulsive about her that drove people away. But all Sierra's friend had said was, "Oh, somebody else already asked to be my partner." Self-injurers take things personally and do not shrug off criticism easily.[45]

Anxiety and Depression

There are generally two main reasons self-injurers cite for why they hurt themselves—to feel less or to feel more. People who have anxiety or depression sometimes feel so full of pain that they are desperate to shut off their feelings. Their thoughts whir. Their hearts race. They cannot catch their breath. They feel about to explode from the intensity of their emotions. According to the Anxiety and Depression Association of America, one in ten teenagers suffers from anxiety. For 10 percent of this group the problem is so crippling that it disrupts their lives.[46]

When they injure themselves, it is as if a safety valve has released some of their feelings. Calmness follows. The emotional pain that they cannot control has become a physical pain that they can control. One patient interviewed for the book *Bodily Harm* said, "During the cutting I feel calm, I feel powerful, and I feel

---

Teen Voice: "Anxiety"

All of us have an inner voice. If we are lucky, this voice speaks kindly to us. More often than not, the voice will not shut up. At the end of the day, the brain spins in circles, recalling each wrong thing you said, or did, or felt. One teen poet wrote this line, a powerful description of the anxiety self-injurers feel: "wracked brain nitpicking every square inch of my body, my mind; all analyzed all the time."[d]

Teen Voice: "Innocent Smile"

In this excerpt of a poem posted on the e-zine *Teen Ink*, the author describes how dissociation feels: "No more joy, no more sadness, no emotion, only madness. I can't see. I don't feel. I can't touch. I don't heal."[e]

---

focused. After self-injury I feel so much relief. . . . My inside pain and feelings are gone."[47]

As terrifying as too much emotion can be, feeling nothing can be even more frightening. Dissociation is a defense mechanism that the brain uses to protect you from trauma or conflict or even boredom. When you dissociate, you mentally detach from events around you. We all dissociate at times without realizing it. Have you ever driven home on a familiar route and pulled into your driveway and realized you have no memory of the drive home? That is dissociation.

Some people are very skilled at disguising their inner pain.

A child who is sexually or physically abused by an adult has little power. Her only escape might be by mentally checking out during the ordeal. In her memoir, *I Know Why the Caged Bird Sings*, Maya Angelou describes how her mother's boyfriend sexually molested her when she was only eight years old. During the assault, Angelou left her mind so completely that she thought she had gone to heaven. When she came to, her abuser was washing her off in the bathtub.[48] Angleou's brain was doing the best it could to protect her from a horrible reality.

Dissociation helps a person survive a trauma, but later this defense mechanism can be a real problem. Even minor stressors can send a person into a mental fog. For example, if a child is beaten whenever he shows anger and he dissociates to escape his fear, this pattern will follow him into adulthood. If he feels irritated at his boss or his wife, he could dissociate. This detachment can vary from a state of numbness to complete amnesia. People who dissociate feel as though they are mentally disintegrating. Self-injury, with its pain and its blood, provides proof that they are still alive.[49] One fifteen-year-old wrote on the blog *LifeSIGNS* that she was so numb she could not cry. Cutting was how she cried. "It would be a great step forward when I can cry again. I am just waiting and fighting for that moment."[50]

Read about It: Speak (New York: Farrar, Straus and Giroux, 1999)

Speak by Laurie Halse Anderson tells the story of Melinda, a freshmen girl who suffers a terrible trauma. Rumors about her spread. Friends abandon her. Classmates whisper behind her back. Melinda concludes that it is easier to just keep her mouth shut because no one really wants to hear the truth anyway.

Since her emotions cannot find voice, they come out in other ways. Melinda bites her lips. She accidentally, on-purpose, cuts her finger during art class. She pulls back her thumbnail until it bleeds. But this temporary pain does not stop her emotional turmoil. Through the kindness of her art teacher and the friendship of a boy, Melinda gradually develops more self-confidence. One day the person who hurt Melinda corners her in a janitor's closet. This time she fights back and with that act of self-empowerment, Melinda finally rediscovers her voice.[f]

Biological Causes

The brain is an intricate, complicated, and mysterious machine. Studies indicate that the biology and chemistry of the brain make certain individuals more vulnerable to self-injury disorder. The opioid system is made up of the neurotransmitters that regulate our feelings of pleasure and pain relief. When the body is injured, opioids are released. One current theory is that people who self-harm are biologically predisposed to receive large bursts of opioids when their bodies are injured. These opioids bring on a rush of euphoria. But when this effect wears off, the person craves it just like any addictive drug.[51] These opioids are the brain's equivalent of heroin.

So, is self-injury addictive? This question continues to be debated and studied. There is not currently enough evidence to prove that self-injury is physiologically addictive. However, the behavior of people who harm themselves is similar to that of people who abuse alcohol and other drugs. Self-injurers and addicts engage in their destructive behavior in order to feel better emotionally and physically. Self-injury, like drugs and alcohol, results in a short-term high. Finally, just like the alcoholic who progresses from needing three drinks a day to six, self-injurers

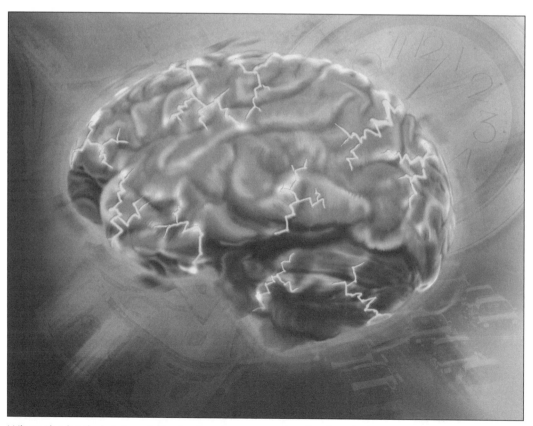

When the body is injured, the brain releases a natural pain relief, similar to heroin.

build up a tolerance and require more frequent and more serious injury to achieve the desired calming effect.[52]

Gwen, a college student, tried to explain the addictive nature of her SI.

I remember getting this high from it. Not necessarily this happy high—but it was a high. It's like that adrenaline rush I was talking about. Like you cut yourself, and your blood pressure would go up, and your heart rate would go faster, and you would get flushed, and it would—there was no pain, and then it would start bleeding, and it'd sting, and then you'd come down from it. It was kind of like this emotional high too, but I don't know—it's more physical. You're feeling so much.[53]

V. J. Turner, the author of *Secret Scars: Uncovering and Understanding the Addiction of Self-Injury*, maintains that even if we do not understand all the neurobiology of SI, the disorder should be treated like an addiction. According to a basic dictionary definition, an addict is someone who devotes herself to something

Movie Review: Thirteen, Directed by Catherine Hardwicke, Produced by Jeffrey Levy-Hinte and Michael London, 2003

The 2003 film *Thirteen* is the story of how Tracy's life spins out of control when she falls under the influence of Evie, the most popular girl in seventh grade. Tracy tries hard to be just like Evie. She dresses provocatively. She drinks and uses drugs. She makes out with boys. And she pulls further and further away from her mother. In a desperate attempt to gain some control over her chaotic life, Tracy goes to the bathroom and cuts herself with a scissor.

Self-injury is just one theme of self-destruction in this film. While the title is *Thirteen* and the two leads are thirteen-year-old girls, the movie is R-rated because of the mature content. But older teens and parents who watch it will see a convincing performance of teenage girls struggling to craft their identity and a mother who is clueless but cares deeply about her daughter. Another interesting note about this movie is that Nikki Reed, the actress who plays bad-girl Evie, cowrote the screenplay when she was only thirteen.

habitually or obsessively. People with SI do this. Turner compares SI with a study on heroin addicts in New York City. The drug addicts become physically dependent on the heroin; they crave it; they obsess about how to get the drug and when to use. Turner recognizes the same patterns in her patients who self-harm.[54] Self-injuring is used to achieve a desired emotional effect—to ramp a person up or to calm a person down. This sounds a lot like the uppers and the downers that drug addicts crave to achieve balance in their lives. People with SI will acknowledge the addictive qualities of their act. Jean Lynch was interviewed for the book *Self-Mutilation*. Lynch admitted that cutting felt good. It was controlled pain that gave her a rush of adrenaline. "Cutting is a drug—it gets you high," she said.[55] Another cutter, Lindsay, echoed Lynch's description of how SI can become habitual. "It really is like an addiction," Lindsay said. "You do it the first time and see how much better you feel. Then when you feel bad again you think, 'Hey, that cutting thing helped.' So you start doing it every time you feel bad."[56] That is how addiction works.

The Wrap-Up

You should now have a picture of who self-injures. They come from every racial group. They can be male or female. They might be on the honor roll or in a juvenile detention center. Why they injure is as varied as what these people look like. Their disorder might be a product of a highly impulsive, overly sensitive person-

Answers and Assistance:
National Alliance on Mental Illness

Not everyone who self-injures has a mental illness, but about half of them do. Self-injury can be a symptom of several disorders including bipolar, depression, and borderline personality disorder. The National Alliance on Mental Illness (NAMI) is the largest grassroots organization in the nation. It provides free mental health referrals through their NAMI helpline. It runs public awareness campaigns and lobbies the government to provide funds for research and programs to support the mentally ill. NAMI's primary goal is to help the sixty million mentally ill Americans lead happier, healthier, and productive lives. Their website is found at www.nami.org.

ality. It might be a coping mechanism that stemmed from childhood trauma. Or it could be that the self-injurers are addicted to the physiological and psychological relief that damage to the body provides. More than likely, a person self-injures because of a complicated combination of reasons.

Although people have different reasons for injuring themselves, the process of the act is remarkably similar for everyone. The next chapter will explore the triggers, the act, and the aftermath of self-harm.

CRIMSON TEARS— THE ACT AND ITS CONSEQUENCES

A person does not wake up one day and decide, *Hey, I think I'll become a self-injurer.* This disorder gradually becomes a habit. Maybe you accidentally injured yourself and discovered that the physical pain diminished your emotional pain. Or perhaps you have a friend who self-injures and you decided to test out this behavior yourself. Possibly you first heard about self-injury in health class and tried it in a moment of stress. Regardless of how the disorder begins, self-injury is a choice that is tripped by an emotional trigger. Once that trigger is sprung, strong feelings follow. Anger, anxiety, and alarm build in the body. Pressure grows and tension tightens. The psychological and physical discomfort is so intense that self-injury seems to be the only option.

The Self-Injury Pattern

The First Trigger

As infants we learn how to calm ourselves. We suck a thumb or a pacifier or cuddle with a blanket. As we grow older, the ways in which we handle life's stresses depends on our personalities and what we have learned from our environment.

When Caroline Kettlewell was in the seventh grade, her science class was examining slides under microscopes. She became fascinated with the splotches of tissue and blood and could not stop thinking about what her own fresh blood would look like under the microscope.[1]

Fifteen-year-old Lucy had been depressed for a long time. She tried to hide it, but one day she looked in the bathroom mirror and no longer recognized herself. Lucy said, "My soul wasn't there. It was just a body to me, and I didn't feel part of it anymore."[2]

Rachel was a high school student when her group of friends turned on her. She withdrew to her room and grew sadder day by day until she felt like her heart would break.[3]

These three individuals chose a similar response to their emotional trigger. Caroline used a Swiss Army knife to saw a gash on her arm in the girls' bathroom of her school. Lucy stood in front of her bathroom mirror and used a razor blade to slice her skin. Rachel yanked a coat hanger from the closet in her bedroom and used it to scratch her arm. Their struggle with self-injury disorder had begun.

The type of stress that serves as the first trigger to self-injury is as unique as the individuals who suffer from SI. For some, like Marie, a thirty-something bank teller, severe mental illness plagued her life. She could not tell you about the first time she harmed herself because she suffers from multiple personality syndrome and cannot remember anything prior to age eighteen. Some alter ego carries her memories of those years.[4]

One too many blows triggered Adam's self-harm. His stepfather verbally abused Adam, whipped him with a belt, and grounded him to his room. The first time Adam cut himself, he was trying to transfer the pain in his head into a pain he could see.[5]

The strain of mental illness like Marie's and physical abuse like Adam's are understandable strains on a young person's psyche. However, for many self-injurers, the first encounter with cutting or burning is triggered by something ordinary—something most people might gripe about or swear about or shed a few tears over.

Chelsea does not remember any particular trauma that led to the first time she cut herself at age fifteen. "I just remember, like, I—I wasn't happy or something and I wanted to see what it would feel like."[6]

Rachel got into an argument with her group of high school friends. They refused to talk to her. They started rumors about her. This social ostracism is an unfortunate part of life for many teenagers, but Rachel reacted differently than other students might. She retreated to her room and took a coat hanger from her closet. "It felt so much better to sit there and scratch myself than to have my heart broke and crying. It eased me. It made me feel better. I was taking it out on my arm as opposed to crying. I felt like I was accomplishing something rather than sitting there crying and being upset for no reason."[7]

Adolescence is a time to test boundaries and take risks. A desire to rebel caused Amy to first burn herself at age fourteen. She was an A student, a Goody Two-shoes and she wanted a different image. "So I determined to be all-out bad. I started smoking and doing a whole bunch of other stuff. Burning was one of my rebellious types of acts."[8]

Emotion is the backdrop to the trigger. Loneliness, anxiety, despair, confusion, anger—whatever the emotion is, it builds and builds. The person cannot or

Musical Message: "Tell-Tale Signs," by Frank Turner, Tape Deck Heart, Interscope, 2013

Intense emotions trigger episodes of self-injury. Frank Turner, British punk rock singer, compares his adult pain from a breakup with a lover to the wounds he made on his own body as a teen. Part of the refrain goes like this: "You know you kind of remind me of scars on my arms that I hid as best I could, that I covered with ink, but in the right kind of light they still bleed through."[a]

In an interview with the *Guardian* in 2014, Turner discussed the self-harm he engaged in as a youth. "Like a lot of people, I feel slightly embarrassed by it—because it's such a concession of weakness. I don't have an enormously high opinion of myself. It's a constant battle not to get too lost in self-criticism, self-loathing." Although Turner is far removed in age from the teenager who carved up his arms, life still dishes out grief and heartache. Age has given him perspective.[b]

does not know how to talk about how she feels. But it is still a big leap from sadness to slicing one's skin. What brings such an act into the mind in the first place?

In *The Tender Cut*, Patricia and Peter Adler pinpointed several ways in which teens get the idea to try self-harm. Prior to the disorder emerging into public awareness in the late 1990s, some self-injurers invented self-injury on their own. Robin was one of these. She began hurting herself as a young kid, without even knowing why. "I hit myself," Robin said. "I hit my face a lot. I didn't understand what was really wrong with it; I didn't understand that it was something odd."[9] She got in trouble all the time from doing things like stapling her fingers. No one had modeled self-injury for Robin. She had not read about it or seen a television show about the disorder. She just hurt herself one day, found it satisfying, and kept on doing it.

Other youth might learn about self-harm from the media. By the late 1990s, television shows and magazines had raised public awareness about this disorder. That exposure led some teens to experiment. Dana remembered that as a teenager she had seen a *Dateline* special about self-injury and read a few magazine articles on the subject. Years later, after a day filled with emotional turmoil, she recalled those stories. But instead of remembering how the news stories had discussed how self-harm had devastated peoples' lives, Dana honed in on the description of the emotional pain the injurers had felt and the relief that cutting gave them. She said, "I was like, Other people have done it; I'll try it. Maybe I'll feel better."[10]

School teaches youth the three Rs, but sometimes kids learn lessons that their teachers never intended. After her health teacher covered a lesson on self-injury, Joanna tucked the information away in a corner of her brain. When the abuse from her stepdad became too hard to deal with, she pulled out that mental file. Joanna gave herself two black eyes, hoping to show her mother the kind of pain she felt on the inside.[11]

What triggers a self-injurer's first time is different for everyone. Perhaps it was an accident. Perhaps it was an experiment. Perhaps the individual decided to try self-harming—just this once. But then she or he does it again. And again.

The Progression

The first time Lisa cut herself, it terrified her. She had argued with her father over the telephone. Enraged, Lisa threw a glass. As she cleaned up the broken glass, she deliberately cut herself. Despite the immediate emotional release she experienced, or perhaps because of it, Lisa was frightened. She did not self-injure again for months.[12]

However, once that initial step has been taken, most people harm themselves again. They find it easier the second time. Alice, a twenty-two-year-old, described how her self-injury progressed. "At first . . . you only do it to a certain level. But as you do it more and more, you get more used to that feeling and more comfortable with doing that to yourself. . . . I was able to cut deeper and with sharper and larger objects."[13]

When Pain Feels Good

Even people who do not self-injure occasionally experience the odd pleasure of pain. Think of the following behaviors in which the pain can be a sort of relief:

- Stretching a sore muscle
- Popping a pimple
- Throwing up when you have the stomach flu
- Sinking into a very hot bathtub
- Diving into a cold pool on a hot day

Alexis, a teenager from a family she describes as completely average, wanted to pierce her belly button and her mother would not permit it. So one day, Alexis pushed a gold stud into the fold of skin on her belly button and pierced it herself. She had not expected the gush of blood or the flood of relief that came with this small act of rebellion. "It just made me feel so much better when I was done . . . everything was okay then—I had control."[14] From a belly ring stud, Alexis progressed to cutting herself with tacks, safety pins, razors, and knives.[15] Often people with SI first hurt themselves with a household object—a butter knife, a broken CD. But as the behavior escalates, they purchase implements just for the purpose of self-harm such as an X-Acto knife or a straight razor.

It is not just the tools self-injurers use that evolve with each act, but also the frequency. Alexis went from harming herself once a week to more than once a day. Anytime she felt, not just bad or sad, but simply felt any emotion at all.[16] Amy, the young rebel, used to hold a metal screw to a lighter flame to heat it up. Then she would hold it against her skin. At first she could only endure the pain a few seconds, but each time she self-harmed, she tried to hold that screw on for longer.[17] She needed to make that sensation last, but the more often Amy burned herself, the less emotional release she felt, so she was compelled to burn herself more frequently and for longer periods of time. The cycle of self-injury had caught her in its endless loop.

The Cycle

Once self-injury is seized on as a coping mechanism, people tend to follow a common pattern. When something triggers a negative emotion, they get the impulse to hurt themselves. Then they fixate on this desire. The urge to injure plays over and over again in a mental loop. Negative thoughts increase negative emotions. Everything that happens around the self-injurer is filtered through a dark lens. What might be innocent behavior on the part of someone else seems designed to hurt.[18] Thoughts and feelings quicken. The self-injurer feels as though he is spinning around in a whirlpool of anxiety and depression and anger.

V. J. Turner, the author of *Secret Scar*, is not only a licensed clinical psychologist but also a woman who suffered from SI for years. She describes the cycle of emotions that can exert so much pressure on a person that she feels absolutely compelled to release the tension.

Sometimes a person's inner pain and rage and frustration are so deep, so unbearable, that there are no words to describe the raging tornado building within her mind and body. An upsetting event happens or an unkind word is said. Then the internal dialogue begins, like a fast-moving train. Turner described her

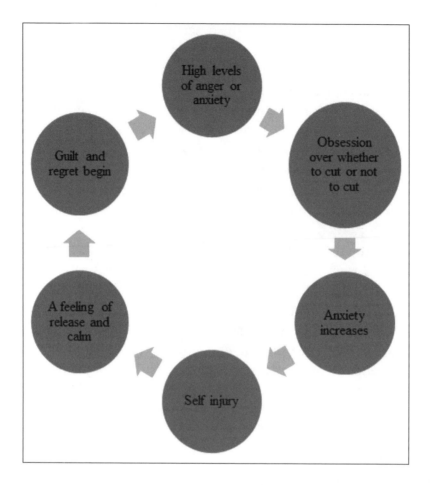

thoughts as obsessing on images and sensations that seem to say to her, "To cut or not to cut, to cut or not to cut, to cut or not to cut . . ."[19]

Books about self-injury, including this book, attempt to explain SI logically, in a step-by-step fashion. However, it is critical to understand that SI is a disorder that is not about logic. Emotions lie at the core of this disease. But the range of emotion that fuels the self-injury cycle covers a broad spectrum.

Feelings That Fuel the Act

Stress

We live in a fast-paced world of high expectations. This can create a pressure cooker of stress for young adults with poor coping mechanisms. Denise Clark Pope, the director of the Stressed-Out Students Project at Stanford University said, "Now more than ever before, pressure for high achievement in school has become a significant risk factor for adolescent mental and physical health, aca-

Read about It: The Luckiest Girl in the World *(New York: Penguin Books, 1998)*

Everyone thinks Katie is so lucky. She's pretty and a top student and a champion ice skater. What no one knows is that Katie has a secret. Sometimes she feels like she's disappearing. The world falls away and she no longer knows where she is. But Katie found a way to make these episodes go away. A snip of the scissors on her arm, a gush of blood, and she's back in the world with more energy to be as perfect as her mother demands.

This novel was written by Steven Levenkron, a therapist who has worked with people who self-injure. The book describes the fictional struggle of Katie Roskova to overcome her increasing dependence on cutting. When Katie falls apart at school one day and is forced to go to therapy, she finally enters into a relationship with an adult she can trust. And Katie learns to use words, instead of scissors, to take back her life.

---

demic integrity and school engagement."[20] The consequences of stress on young people have led to an explosion of reactions: anxiety, depression, and cheating scandals. College students abuse attention deficit disorder drugs such as Ritallin and Adderall in order to pull all-night study cram sessions. The mantra of success at all costs has a high cost indeed: eating disorders, sleep disorders, and self-injury.

Christina is an example of a stressed out teen. She is a junior at a suburban high school and carries a 3.8 GPA. On a typical day she rises at 5:30 in the morning for water polo practice. Then she attends classes from 8:00 to 3:00. Her course load is tough: honors chemistry, honors history, and honors English. After school, she must work with her chemistry lab partner to prepare for the next day's exam. After that she goes to symphony practice where Christina plays the flute. She finally returns home at 6:00, exhausted, but she still has to study. She can't seem to concentrate and this makes her anxious. If she gets less than A− in chemistry, she won't reach her college admission goals. The more anxious Christina feels, the less she can concentrate. She is desperate for something to break this cycle of stress.[21]

Anger

Leila described herself as a perfectionist. She grew up in a wealthy family, was a musical prodigy, and a chess champion. Her parents attended all her recitals and school functions and cheered her on. But when Leila became a college student, life began to sour. She alternated between depression and anger, and when she was angry, she hurt herself. "My anger feels white-hot, frustration and vicious," Leila wrote in her diary. She had fantasies of attacking whomever she was angry at. She used a razor blade to cut her legs and her chest.[22] Leila's life seemed perfect to an outsider, but on the inside she seethed.

Other self-injurers experience anger for reasons that anyone could understand. Bonnie had a history of sexual abuse that left behind a minefield of rage. She had flashbacks that left her with an anger that she did not know what to do with. Many females do not know how to handle anger. While society accepts male expressions of rage, women are discouraged from hostile displays of emotion. They are taught to internalize their anger. Connie, a nineteen-year-old college student, said that self-injury was the only thing that calmed her down. "I wanted to punch walls and stuff like that, but I didn't want to be so loud about it. So it was taking anger out on myself."[23]

This self-directed anger is a common refrain in the stories of females with SI. Darcy was a teenager from a divorced family. Self-harm was a way of keeping her anger at her parents in check. "I don't like to be upset with other people, and I don't like to act out upset on other people. So if I'm really upset with what somebody else has done, I'll tell them about it, but it's not to the extent I'd like to. So then I cut myself, and I'm not upset anymore."[24] A quick slice across the skin, and no more anger.

Sadness and Self-Loathing

Clinical depression is a serious mental illness. It causes a persistent, overwhelming feeling of sadness that interferes with life. But you don't have to be a diagnosed depressive to experience loneliness and despair at some point in life. When sadness creeps up on some people, they get rid of it by hurting themselves. Alice is one of those people. During her own birthday party one year, she felt like no one was paying her any attention. Her brother's friends were over, and they monopolized everyone's attention. Then a girl snapped at Alice. She said she was "just feeling really hated and lonely. And so I think that feeling really down about yourself and then having somebody say something really mean to you or treat you badly, that just sort of sends you spiraling into an even worse depression than you

Could You Be a Self-Injurer?

If you are concerned that you might suffer from self-injury disorder, you should seek help from a professional. The following questions are drawn from several sources to help you gauge how serious your self-harm might be.

1. Do you deliberately harm yourself to cope with your feelings?
2. Do you have more than one method of self-injury?
3. Do you feel no pain when you self-harm?
4. Do you self-injure alone?
5. Do you wear clothes to cover your wounds and scars?
6. Do you sometimes feel that you are so far gone that only self-injury will reset you back to normal?
7. Do you feel a sense of release when you are done self-injuring?
8. Do you feel emotionally numb?
9. Do you have episodes when you feel extremely angry or anxious?
10. Do you get a high from self-injuring?

If you recognized yourself in three or more of these statements, it is time to seek help. These behaviors are common to people with self-injury disorder.

already are in."[25] While her birthday party continued, Alice went into the bathroom and cut herself. Her sadness went away. For a while.

Numbness

Victims of past trauma will sometimes turn to self-injury when they are on the verge of dissociating. While this state of "spacing out" helped them survive abuse earlier in their lives, it is an acutely uncomfortable state to function in on a daily basis. One self-injurer described how once during a spell of dissociation, she just sat and stared at her own hands as though they were something separate from her body. Another woman said when she cuts herself, she looks at her body as though it is a carcass of meat hanging on a hook. The sight of blood brings this woman back to her senses.[26] The self-harm is sort of an on-off switch for those who dissociate. Self-harm can pull them back into reality.[27]

This was the situation for Marissa. She cut when she felt blank, and the pain brought her out of this trance-like state. Judy cut herself when she could not bear not feeling anything. "It's better to feel pain than nothing, and when I asked my friends if they had ever felt like they couldn't feel anything, they would say, 'What are you talking about?' So I felt weird."[28]

While some people self-injure to escape the numbness of dissociation, others seek that emotionless state. Any emotion is too much. This was the case for Lindsay. She began to cut when she was frightened or felt like she had no control. But soon she self-injured when any sort of negative emotion entered her brain. "I did it when I was afraid my friends didn't like me anymore. I did it when I was worried. I did it if I got a bad grade. I even did it if I had cavities. As soon as I began to feel bad about something the thought popped into my head and . . . I just kept thinking that the sooner I cut the bad feeling would go away so why wait?"[29]

The Act

Some people experience such an intense urge to harm themselves that they do it impulsively wherever they are. However, most people have a preferred method, place, and time.

Where and When

The evening is the time of day most people self-injure, in part because the frustrations of the day have built up and finally, when the day is almost done, they have time to reflect on how they feel about what happened. Wendy was a high-achieving graduate student. In the evening hours she replayed her perceived *failures* of that day, and cut to punish herself for not achieving what she believed she should have. Jane, another college student, felt exhausted by the end of the day. She was physically less capable of handling stress by that hour and self-injury helped her manage her anxiety.[30]

Evening is also the time of day that offers more privacy and opportunity. People are alone in their rooms, often unable to sleep as they think endlessly about what happened that day. Self-injury can be a sort of sleeping pill for those who cannot turn off the mental loop that plays incessantly in their brain. Hannah, a college student, made self-injury as routine as brushing her teeth. "I'd read for a while, and then I'd injure, and then I'd go to bed. Most of the time it was when I was upset, but then it just became so routine that I just did it every night regardless of what I was feeling. It was just part of what I did."[31]

Privacy is critical for the act of self-injury. The majority of people prefer to do it at home. Not only do they have more control over their surroundings, but the emotions that precede self-injury are greater when a person is alone and has time to think and feel without distraction. The floor of a dark closet. By the light of a computer monitor in a dark bedroom. A room in the basement. The bathtub. However, if an individual is desperate, a public bathroom stall will do the job.[32]

Tool Kit

Usually, when people first begin to self-injure, they make do with what is at hand. In high school, Crystal would punch her fist through mirrors or windows following fights with her mother. After a birthday party that made her miserable, Alice used a nail clipper.[33]

However, over time, many self-injurers put together a kit. Some are precise about sterilizing their equipment; others do not care about possible infection. Eileen stored broken beer bottles, razor blades, and chipped pottery in a Tupperware container in her bedroom. Mandy staunched the blood from her cuts with the same dirty towel every time she cut, never washing it. Janice prepared to harm herself with the precision of a doctor before surgery. She laid out Band-Aids, put a clean blade on her X-Acto knife, and sterilized her skin before and after the act.[34]

The tool kit and the rituals involved in setting up and cleaning up can be as gratifying as the actual act for some people. Katy was a college student who prepared for every act of self-harm very deliberately. She shut her blinds and turned on a bedside lamp. She changed into a tank top. She opened packets of sterilized gauze in the same precise order every time. Then she cleansed her skin. After she cut, Katy followed a similarly detailed clean-up routine.[35] Tamara, a woman who began to cut in her early twenties, found a satisfying sense of control in preparing for the act. She laid out the items of her tool kit—razor blades, cotton balls, a towel. She pressed the blade against her skin to measure the length she would cut. During the routine, she asked herself questions. Should she stop? Is there anyone she could call? She made a light scratch on the surface of her skin and waited to see if that was enough. If not, she continued. Each time she self-injures, the ritual is the same.[36]

Focus

During the cut or burn or break, people concentrate on different things. For some, the emotion they feel is at the core of the act. Lois was a college student who deliberately concentrated on all her sad feelings. As she lay on her bed weeping, her depression welled up, and right at the peak of the emotion, she would cut her arm with a razor. Hannah, another college student, repeated one thought in her mind over and over. This thought became a mantra for her injury.[37]

For other self-injurers it is not the emotion that preoccupies them. It is the blood. One teen whom Patricia and Peter Adler discuss in *The Tender Cut* viewed her blood as her friend. She said, "My own blood isn't going to look back in my face and say 'You're stupid. Why are you doing this? You're worthless.'"[38]

What role blood plays in SI is the subject of research. One study questioned a group of college students who cut themselves. Eighty-five percent of them said that seeing blood during a self-injury episode helped them calm down. Half of them said it made them "feel real."[39] One female interviewed in a different study was so numb that bleeding was the only way she could express emotion. "The blood told me I was alive, that I could feel. I needed to see those bad feelings bleed away. Also I couldn't cry, and bleeding was a different form of crying."[40]

In the study of college students, those who valued the sight of blood cut an average of eight times more frequently than those who reported that bleeding was not an important part of their self-injury. The students who needed to bleed were also more likely to have symptoms of bulimia and borderline personality disorder.[41]

At this point researchers have more questions than answers about why blood plays this role for some people. What is the mechanism by which the blood helps calm a person down? Our bodies operate with an automatic nervous system that has two parts—the sympathetic and the parasympathetic. When we are under a threat, our sympathetic nervous system accelerates the heart rate, ramps up the blood pressure, and constricts our blood vessels. The parasympathetic system has the opposite effect. Some studies show that people with blood phobias have a big spark in the sympathetic nervous system response when they see blood. One hypothesis about SI is that perhaps people who like to see blood when they self-harm, experience a similar jolt in the sympathetic nervous system, but this jolt is quickly followed by a rebound response of the parasympathetic nervous system. Therefore, at the sight of blood, the tension and anxiety they feel is replaced by relaxation and calm.[42] More research needs to be conducted on this topic, but clearly blood has great power for many self-injurers.

Release

With the slice of a blade or flame held to the flesh, self-injurers experience an intense release. Janice described it as "a total rush. It's like a high. It's almost like doing a drug."[43] For other people the relief was there, but it was not totally pleasant. Brooke felt her heart beat quicken and her body flush. The sting of her cut sharpened her awareness. Her anger, fear, and sadness poured out of her along

Musical Message: "Hurt," by Nine-Inch Nails, The Downward Spiral, Interscope Records, 1994

This song "Hurt" is about consequences and regret. The opening line is "I hurt myself today/To see if I still feel/I focus on the pain/The only thing that's real." The song was recorded by Trent Reznor and the band Nine-Inch Nails in 1994. The song has been rerecorded by other groups, including most famously by country and western star Johnny Cash, who called it the best antidrug song he had ever heard. Self-harm takes many forms, including alcohol and drug abuse, something both Cash and Reznor battled.[c]

Reznor wrote this song when he was going through a period in life when he hated the world and had turned inward. He was able to channel his feelings into music. "I found I could turn that into something. Instead of punching the wall and having my hand hurt, I could write it down. Strangely things came out of it that seemed to have this catharsis. There was a beautiful element to it and it made me feel good."[d]

---

with her blood and sometimes she wept.[44] Katherine, a college student, tried to drag out each self-injury as long as possible because she enjoyed the release. However, as soon as the act was over, guilt set in.[45]

The sensation that comes with self-injury can be sensual for some people. One woman posted this on an Internet forum: "Don't encourage anyone to do this but tonight I cut and that crap felt like an orgasm."[46] It is the release that causes this feeling, the heightening of tension and its rapid falling away. One college student posted as much on a social media site. She said, "I don't wanna compare it to this, but it was sort of like orgasmatic, if that makes any sense at all. Like you would do it and finally feel it and feel the release."[47]

The relief from tension and unwanted emotions is what reinforces the self-injurious behavior. Reinforcement is a basic principle of animal behavior. If the consequences that follow a behavior get us to repeat that behavior, then we have reinforced it. The process is called negative reinforcement when the behavior helps you get rid of something unpleasant. For example, you might feel depressed if your boyfriend breaks up with you. Then perhaps you cut yourself, and afterward you feel less depressed. According to the principle of negative reinforcement, you

The pressure of high-stakes competition can cause some athletes to self-injure.

will cut again next time you feel sad. Positive reinforcement is a similar process, only the consequence is something you want, not something you want to get rid of. If you feel excitement or euphoria after harming yourself, you will be more likely to repeat that behavior so that you can feel those sensations again.[48]

The End of the Act

Two factors determine when a person ends an episode of self-injury: the amount of damage done to the body or the feelings the person is experiencing. Some

Running on Empty: Olympian Kelly Holmes

In 2004 British track and field athlete Kelly Holmes won two gold medals. As she stood on the podium and bowed her head to receive her medals, no one knew that the pressure of training for the Olympic Games had led Holmes to self-injure.[e]

One year earlier, Holmes had injured her calf and training was agony. She locked herself in the bathroom and turned on the faucet so no one could hear her cry. Then Holmes, age thirty-four at the time, spotted a pair of scissors. She used the scissors to cut her left arm, one slice for each day she had been injured. "I felt I was punishing myself but at the same time I felt a sense of release that drove me to do it again and again. I knew deep inside that I wouldn't go any further. The whole episode was nothing more than a cry of despair."[f]

While Holmes eventually sought professional help to deal with her emotional strain, in 2012 she did admit to self-injuring after retiring from professional racing.

people count their cuts. Leith was a young man who believed the number nine had special importance for him and so he always cut in groups of nine. However, he said that someday he might try to cut himself one hundred times. Ingrid cut herself in a series of five slashes. After each set of five, she would stop, assess her feelings, and decide whether she needed to continue or not. Some self-injurers might have a favorite number or want to cut more than they did during the last episode while others must see blood.[49]

One anonymous teen described slicing her (or his) wrist nineteen times. The skin was tissue-paper thin. As this teen wept in the shower, it felt so good to see "striking red drops swirl with colorless pools of water." According to this young person, although the crimson tears ran down the drain, the smell of blood and soap and sadness could not be washed away.[50]

For some people it is not the blood or the number of wounds that tells them when to stop a self-injury episode. Instead their feelings are the signal. What those feelings are differs from person to person. The sensation might be pain. These individuals do not stop cutting or punching or burning until physical pain replaces the rage or despair that triggered their actions. Cindy, a nineteen-year-old, explained that she went into a kind of daze when she self-injured. But the pain "kind of wakes you up."[51] Other people know they have gone far enough when a sense of calm falls over them. Katy was one of these people. "If I was

Movie Review: Short Term 12, Directed by Destin Daniel Cretton, Animal Kingdom Traction Media, 2013

The central figure of this 2013 movie is Grace, the supervisor of an adolescent group home. When a new girl named Jaden arrives, she forces Grace to deal with issues in her own difficult past. Grace and Jaden form a connection based on their mutual passion as artists and their shared experience as cutters. Grace's boyfriend and coworker, Mason, tries to get Grace to confide in him, but she has spent years denying her abusive upbringing, and this proves a difficult habit to break. However, with the insights she gains from her relationships with the struggling teens, Grace finds some emotional peace. *Short Term 12* is tragic, funny, and uplifting.

angry or I was feeling too much, if I needed to calm down, if I needed to control it, if I needed to feel, I'd stop when I felt something."[52] Then there are the self-injurers who hurt themselves until they reach a point of physical and emotional exhaustion and they simply collapse.[53]

However, you do not always get to choose when an episode of self-injury ends. Someone could walk in and discover you in the middle of cutting yourself. Danielle was a thirty-something-year-old mother of three. She lost consciousness one night during a self-injury episode and a neighbor came in and discovered her.[54] You might cut deeper than you intended and not be able to staunch the bleeding. You might be forced to seek help in the emergency room. You might wind up being committed to a psychiatric hospital. No matter what brings the episode of self-injury to an end, eventually, perhaps not until hours or even days later, the self-injurer begins to feel guilt, shame, and regret. And for many people those emotions cause the cycle to begin all over again.

Wrap-Up

Self-injury follows a pattern: first comes the trigger, then the cycle of negative thoughts and emotions, followed by the act and its aftermath. The sensation of release reinforces the behavior. It is important to understand that this cycle of self-injury is a coping mechanism. It is unhealthy and self-destructive, but people

Answers and Assistance: Who Can You Call?

When your urge to self-injure is triggered, pick up the phone and call someone. A trusted friend, your therapist, a pastor. But what if you have no one to call? What if self-injury is your shameful secret? There are twenty-four-hour crisis hotlines you can call for help.

The people who answer the phones are trained to listen to people going through a rough time. Be prepared for the person on the phone to ask questions to find out if you are suicidal or not.

800-273-TALK (8255)—Mental Health America (www.nmha.org)

800-SUICIDE (784-2433)

800-334-HELP (4357)

800–799-SAFE (7233)—domestic violence hotline

866-4-U-Trevor—for GLBTQ youth (www.thetrevorproject.org)

877-332-7333—teen hotline

800799-4889—deaf hotline

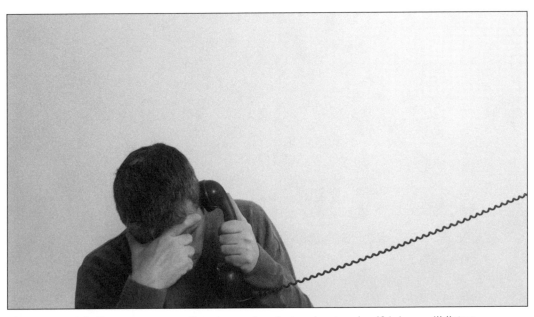

There are crisis lines you can call and people who understand self-injury will listen.

do feel better immediately after injuring. However, later—maybe minutes, maybe hours, maybe days—shame and guilt and disgust will kick in. Then the negative thoughts result in bad feelings. The tension grows and the cycle repeats itself.

This self-destructive pattern will continue until you learn how to break it. Some people think the Internet is a powerful recovery tool that can help self-injurers who often suffer in isolation. However, others believe that chat rooms and social media actually cause this disorder to spread. The next chapter explores self-injury disorder in the cyber world.

SELF-INJURY IN CYBERSPACE

Self-injury is an act usually done is isolation. Most people keep this behavior a secret, sure that no one could possible understand why they would willingly scar their own flesh. The Internet is changing this norm. Now people can make connections in the cyber world while keeping the fact that they self-harm a secret in their real-world relationships.

Today the average American youth spends as many as eight and one-half hours a day using electronic media.[1] Between December of 2000 and June of 2012, Internet use by young people increased by 566 percent.[2] More than 80 percent of American youth between the ages of twelve and seventeen report using the Internet and more than 50 percent of these kids log on daily.[3] They do their homework online, buy products over the Internet, and read e-zines and e-books. However, for most young people, including self-injurers, the most important function of the Internet is to connect socially.

The web provides both passive and active ways for people with self-injury disorder to reach out electronically. Websites are loaded with information about what causes self-injury, how to spot its symptoms, and where to seek help. These sites are often run by recovering self-injurers or members of the medical community. Reading about other people's experiences can help self-injurers feel validated. They are often surprised to learn that they are not the only people in the world who self-harm.

Carlie began to self-injure in the early 1990s when she was only thirteen, using plastic knives to saw at her arms. Neither social media nor online forums existed for Carlie then. So when she was in her twenties and first typed in "cuts self" in an Internet search engine, she was relieved to find that there was a name for what she did. And that other people cut themselves too. "It made me feel a lot better. It made me feel sad that there were so many people that felt so bad, but that made me feel better that I wasn't the only one."[4]

Musical Message: "Beyond the Surface" by Kutless, Hearts of the Innocent, *Capitol Christian Music Group*, 2006

When the Christian rock band Kutless recorded their album *Hearts of the Innocent*, they had a mission. They wanted to let the older generation known that modern youth were struggling. According to lead singer Andrew Morrison, if adults do not teach the younger generation how to manage their emotions, "when life becomes difficult or throws a curveball their way, they end up just turning to other things. Whether it be illegal activity, or self-mutilation."

The lyrics to Kutless's single "Beyond the Surface" communicate the alienation and isolation people feel, even in a world where they can remain socially connected 24/7: "I've been hiding, hiding for so long right behind my digital mask. I've been trying to be someone I'm not." Consistent with the band's mission, this song offers a positive message. The listener is urged to put the knife away and not to let fear get in the way of change.[a]

Range of Internet Use

The Internet provides both passive and active ways for people with self-injury disorder to reach out electronically. Some people might just want to learn more about their own behavior, whereas others want to personally connect with other people.

Passive Participation

You probably use the Internet frequently to look up the weather report or to research information for a school assignment or to get the latest news or sports results. According to the website Tech Made Easy, in January of 2014 there were 861,379,000 active websites.[5] And that statistic changes every second. Websites are chock-full of statistics, expert opinions, and the latest research on every topic conceivable, including SI.

The most basic way that self-injurers use the Internet is to read information on websites. This is passive because while viewers can read the text and look at pictures, they do not have to respond to this information. These websites are often written by psychological or medical professionals or people who work in therapeutic settings. Websites contain information about the causes of SI, how to tell the difference between SI and suicidal behavior, the history of the disorder, and more.

Another passive form of Internet use is to read the online journals of people who post their experiences with SI. Often these sites take less of an academic approach to the disorder and more of a personal and emotional tone, and they frequently include artwork or poetry. One self-injurer who was interviewed in *The Tender Cut* said that while she did not feel good the first time she encountered self-injury websites when she was only a middle school student, she did feel validated.[6]

Active Participation

For people not content to just read about other's experiences, the Internet also provides the opportunity for interaction. One form this type of cyber community takes is message boards that post different topics, giving readers a place where they can digitally vent. For example, "The Unofficial How Do You Feel Right Now" is a conversation strand on Safe Haven, the message board of the website Self-Injury.net. Sample responses show the range of experiences that self-injurers go through: "Scared." "Okay enough." "Alone and Misunderstood." "I feel real angry and confident—like don't mess with me." People who post on these threads can interact with each other. One person posted, "i want to kill myself . . . i went up the road and tried to jump in front of a bus but was too scared." Other users urged this individual to go to the hospital or call a suicide hotline.[7]

Online self-injury groups have surpassed message boards in popularity. Anyone can read the posts on a public forum, but users can also apply for membership and join. Membership gives them access to more detailed information about other users' profiles. In these cyber communities, a self-injurer can disclose her secrets without the excruciating struggle that such an act takes in the real world. The people who join a self-injury group understand the experience of self-harm. There is no need to explain, justify, or hide. And there are many groups so a person can shop around until she finds the online group that offers the right kind of community. Often people join more than one, which is what Marissa, a depressed middle-aged mother, did. "The depression group," she said, "that's constantly active, and it's international enough that there is somebody there in the middle of the night, so if I am having a really tough night, anytime, there is somebody from Australia or New Zealand, or waking up . . . there is always somebody there to help me through the night."[8]

Online groups fall on a spectrum. Some are highly regulated and focused on recovery. These groups are often connected to treatment centers that work with people who suffer from SI and are hosted by professionals. Words or images that could trigger a desire to self-injury are banned. Recovery is the focus of these groups, and most of them make that clear in their posting rules. Users are only allowed to post their feelings about self-injury, not how they do it, and they must be committed to giving up the behavior. If someone violates these rules, then other group members privately complain to the moderator and the situation is also dealt with in private. These recovery-focused online groups are small and tightly knit with a consistent group of regular members who post comments.[9]

On the opposite end of the spectrum are the groups that embrace self-harm as a lifestyle choice. There are similar groups for other abusive behaviors, including anorexia and bulimia. People who are members of these hard-core groups often compare their behavior to alcohol and drug use, maintaining that SI is healthier. They argue that self-injury is a coping mechanism without the chemically addictive and damaging consequences of alcohol and other drugs. These people insist that their bodies are their own, and, therefore, no one should pass judgment on how they deal with life's stressors. One person who posted to a pro-SI site wrote, "Cutting is the only thing that likes me right now. And it's not killin' me yet, and definitely not killing me as bad as being anorexic is. And it's my way out. Nobody has to know. It's just between me and the box cutter, or the exacto knife, or the scissors."[10]

The most common online SI groups fall in the middle of these two extremes. These sites appeal to people who were too easily triggered by the pro-SI groups but too stifled by the highly regulated groups. They offer a cyber community that recognizes that SI is a negative, potentially dangerous coping mechanism that people should give up; however, these groups do not believe in condemning people who slip up and self-harm.[11]

Sites with chat rooms provide the most immediate interaction. Users are notified when others are online, and these chat rooms operate twenty-four hours a day so people can talk to each other in real time. With webcams people can even see and be seen by people with whom they are having a conversation.[12] The Internet has opened a private door for self-injurers. They control who to talk to, when to talk, and what to say. If the conversation goes in a direction they do not desire, they can just shut off their computers.

Despite that ability to shut off the technology, controversy exists among the mental health community about whether the vast information and instant communication of the Internet is more helpful or harmful to people with self-injury disorder. In 2013, researchers analyzed twenty-one studies that dealt with the impact of the Internet on people who self-harmed. The results were inconclusive. Nine studies showed positive benefits and twelve showed negative effects. Some studies showed both.[13]

Positive Features of the Cyber World

The Internet is anonymous. Many youth report that they are more likely to share private information with strangers online than face-to-face.[14] The Internet can serve as a virtual support group. Teens under stress can express their feelings

Online forums can be a place where teens can anonymously give and get advice about self-injury.

without worry about being judged by people they will see every day. Their emotions seem more normal when they realize that many other people feel similarly. One review of over three thousand posts on an informal Internet support forum showed that 28 percent of posts were from people seeking support and understanding.[15] Josh, a frequent poster to one online group said, "What I get out of the group is just a sense of community, a chance to really express my true self. . . . We are all connected. . . . If one of us hurts, we all hurt."[16] Some studies indicate that this sense of community that Josh described does help. The greater the number of posts created and received in the first two months that a self-injurer participated in an online forum, the less distress he or she expressed in posts by the third month of forum use.[17]

The rapid pace of intimate connections might be one reason self-injurers find the web helpful. As this book has indicated in earlier chapters, people who self-harm have intense emotions, and they are often isolated in their suffering. But once someone posts a message online, they receive floods of responses. Everyone is in that chat room for the same reason—to share emotional experiences. A woman named Bonnie described the way these cyber relationships began: "It's a lot easier to talk to these people online because they don't see you, because you don't have to beat around the bush. The terms you use or the way you explain what happened—you don't have to tiptoe around these people because they've all been there, they know exactly what you're saying."[18]

Peers offer support to each other and suggestions for positive ways to cope with their emotions. In one 2006 study, researchers reported that about 40 percent of posts dealt with giving and receiving informal support. Here is an example of the exchange between two teens, strangers but united by a common struggle.

"I hadn't cut since Wednesday . . . on Thursday my bf dumped me and today, Friday night, I cut again . . . I still am and I can't stop."[19]

Less than an hour later, someone responded.

> That really sucks that He dumped you and I know how you feel. . . . You may feel like hell now but time will heal things and it will get Better. . . . Try to distract yourself by Listening to Music or going for a Run or doing something outside or hanging out with a friend or family. . . . I'm sorry if my advice isn't that Great but most of it is what I wish I said to myself when I went through the same kinda situation. Good Luck . . . and if you ever need to talk I'm here.[20]

Because the web is such a vast network, there are so many self-injury groups that it takes time to find one that fits. Some forums are single-issue groups and only want members who self-harm. Others might be multi-issue groups where members can post about depression, an eating disorder, abuse, or self-injury.

Patricia and Peter Adler's research revealed that people searched until they found an online community that matched their needs in terms of how big it was, the average age of the people who posted, and how often people posted. Even if it took a while, once people found a community that matched their needs, the group identity became part of their own identity and was very important to them.[21]

When the Adlers interviewed Erica, she was a college student. She was an incest survivor, having been sexually abused by her brother when she was only seven years old, and she had been self-injuring since the age of twelve. Erica transitioned from scratching herself with toothpicks to cutting herself with blades. She explained to the Adlers why an online community was so beneficial for her. "You've been there; you know what it's like. I have traits in common with other members of the community; being sexually abused; being a perfectionist, having an eating disorder. . . . Like everything they say on those websites is completely me . . . I just happen to fit. So it makes me feel more connected to the community as a member."[22]

This connectedness with other people is critical for many self-injurers. Remember, these are individuals who may live an outwardly normal life, but then go home at the end of the day, shut their doors, and hurt themselves. Or they might be people whose self-injury is so extreme that they cannot interact in society and have closeted themselves at home in isolation. Several studies indicate that people with disorders that society does not approve of, such as SI, identify more strongly with online groups and they are important components of these peoples' identities.

Help Yourself

● Self-injury can foster depression and feelings of worthlessness. The worse you feel about yourself, the more likely you are to self-injure. Take a minute and find the good in you with this brief exercise.

- In your opinion, what are your three best qualities?
- In the opinion of three people you like and respect, what are your three best qualities? Do you agree or disagree with the qualities these people picked?
- What is one positive thing you heard about yourself that you know is true?

Read these statements out loud to yourself every morning and every evening.

Teens also posted about events in their personal lives that triggered their desire to cut and their fears about the power self-injury had over their lives. Researchers concluded that the teens on the websites they observed used these online forums the same way someone might use a trusting relationship—to share stories, voice opinions, give advice.[23]

The Risks of the Internet

While these results might sound positive, they do not provide a complete picture of SI in the digital world. Not everyone joins an online group in order to get help. A review published in 2013 in the *Public Library of Science* journal found that while posts focus on empathy and compassion, they do not stress recovery or prevention. In fact, 18 percent of people who posted in online forums admitted that they were at least somewhat interested in finding a suicide partner, and over 14 percent were online in search of better ways to hurt themselves. Additionally, over 9 percent of posts dealt with ways to conceal self-harm.[24]

The Internet can become a powerful teacher and friend, but not always a beneficial one. Several studies reviewed for the analysis in the *Public Library of Science* article found that vast majorities of forum users, 59–80 percent, first encountered self-injury through the Internet.[25] Additionally, the Internet can further isolate some socially awkward youth. A study by Carnegie Mellon University suggested that heavy use of the Internet causes isolation, loneliness, and depression. The more time you spend online, the less time you spend talking to friends and family. Superficial online relationships are easier than the face-to-face personal ones.[26]

There is also the danger that when youth view too many images and stories of self-harm, this can legitimize the behavior. Matthew Lorber, the director of child and adolescent psychiatry at Lenox Hill Hospital in New York City, said that chat rooms can lead young people to conclude that self-injury is normal. "I've observed this in my own practice," Lorber said. "A teen told me she went to a chat room on cutting, where basically a lot of teens were acting as if it were cool and no big deal. The Internet also provides access to suicidal content, like how to cut or kill yourself, and certainly that information is readily available."[27] Lorber's concern is supported by one study that found that out of three hundred posts on a self-injury chat room, 9 percent were about ways to self-injure. Users also swapped tips on how to conceal their wounds and scars.[28] While the web can provide support to lonely self-injurers, clearly, some people are searching for something else.

Diseases spread when sick people come into close contact, and researchers have long believed that behaviors are catchy too, through something called "social contagion." This is a process by which behaviors are transmitted from one per-

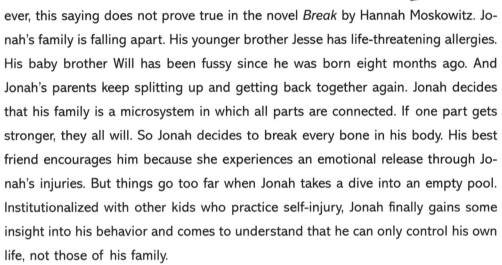

Read about It: Break *(New York: Simon Pulse, 2009)*

There is an old adage that when a person breaks a bone, it grows back stronger. However, this saying does not prove true in the novel *Break* by Hannah Moskowitz. Jonah's family is falling apart. His younger brother Jesse has life-threatening allergies. His baby brother Will has been fussy since he was born eight months ago. And Jonah's parents keep splitting up and getting back together again. Jonah decides that his family is a microsystem in which all parts are connected. If one part gets stronger, they all will. So Jonah decides to break every bone in his body. His best friend encourages him because she experiences an emotional release through Jonah's injuries. But things go too far when Jonah takes a dive into an empty pool. Institutionalized with other kids who practice self-injury, Jonah finally gains some insight into his behavior and comes to understand that he can only control his own life, not those of his family.

son to another. Since there is substantial evidence that behaviors such as fashion, eating disorders, and even suicide, can be spread through social contagion, some researchers speculate that SI can too, especially in the age of the Internet and 24/7 access to media.[29]

It is not only unregulated self-injury forums that concern mental health professionals. YouTube has been the fastest growing video-sharing website since it was developed in 2005. Because teens and young adults have both the highest rates of SI and spend more time online than any other age group, a team of Canadian researchers started watching YouTube too, and what they discovered has raised an alarm.[30]

The team searched YouTube with the key words *self-injury* and *self-harm* and conducted an analysis of the one hundred most-watched videos. The researchers' findings were published in the *Journal of the American Academy of Pediatrics* in 2011. Most of the videos had no viewer age restriction, and more than half did not have trigger warnings to alert self-injurers that the images might make them want to self-harm. Most of the videos had a neutral purpose and did not either encourage or discourage self-injury. The tone of most of the clips was either educational or depressed. Sixty-four percent of the videos showed photographs

Youth often model behavior they see online, including self-injury.

of self-injury, predominately cutting, and the majority of the injuries were classified as moderate. Some of these movies featured characters and some did not, but they all had been viewed millions of times. The noncharacter videos were viewed more often, were rated more favorably, and had more graphic SI content than did the character videos. Music and graphics were woven artistically through the noncharacter videos, and this raised the researchers' concern that these videos might entertain and even normalize SI for some youth. These scientists concluded that more research needs to be done on what effect watching these YouTube clips has on young people.[31]

If youth learn about self-harm on Internet blogs and chat rooms, if they view YouTube clips about celebrities who cut or burn, and if they know kids in school who hurt themselves, this can prime youth to try behaviors they may never have considered. Social learning theory suggests that people learn best from copying models.[32]

Blogger and columnist Michelle Malkin received a letter from a mother who was concerned about her fourteen-year-old daughter. The girl had a 4.0 GPA, a loving family, and a lot of friends. Four of these friends were cutters. The counselor at the girls' school said that 70 percent of the teens she worked with cut or knew someone who did. Self-injury has become almost a fad in some corners of the nation.[33]

#Cut4Bieber

In June 2013, an anonymous person tweeted that people should post pictures of themselves cutting. This was a mock protest that was making fun of pop star Justin Bieber's trouble with substance abuse. In the original tweet the anonymous poster wrote, "See if we can get some little girls to cut themselves." The hashtag #Cut4Bieber began to trend, garnering more than twenty-six thousand hits in twelve hours. There was an onslaught of self-harm photos and many were outraged that people had treated a topic as serious as self-harm so flippantly.[b]

In 1999 the parents of fourteen-year-old Joel Evans from Mill Valley, California, noticed a red indentation on his neck. He made some casual excuse and his parents did not question him further. One day, his mother came home and could not find Joel anywhere. Then she saw a shadow in the window of his bedroom. Joel had hung himself with the mini-blind. The doctors ruled it as suicide, but his parents did not believe this. Later they learned that there was a trend going on among the teens Joel's age. It was called space monkey or the choking game. It is a suffocation game that gives the user a temporary high. The Evans' are sure their son learned about the game online.[34] While this choking game does not fit all the criteria of self-harm, it is an example of how the Internet can be a vehicle to spread self-destructive behavior.

Caitlin Scafati was another fourteen-year-old from California. She was overweight and had trouble adjusting to high school. Once when Caitlin was snacking on a doughnut, a boy teased her about her size. A girl took a picture of Caitlin in her swimming suit and hung it in the locker room. Caitlin turned to her computer for comfort. She googled anorexia and cutting and learned that people use these methods to deal with their emotions. She started to cut her arms and legs, and she stopped eating. In online chat rooms she found other youth who had eating disorders and self-injured. Through these chat rooms, Caitlin learned tips on how to stave off hunger by drinking lots of water or giving her food to her dog. Other online posters gave Caitlin suggestions for how to hide her self-inflicted wounds.[35]

Professionals in the medical field recognize the potential harm online communication poses to self-injurers. Dr. Thomas Andrew, a pediatrician and chief medical examiner from New Hampshire, says that the Internet pushes everything to the extreme. He said that we live in an I-dare-you culture.[36] Kids see things online and try things they normally would not do.

Photographs of blood or fresh scars can be a trigger for some self-injurers.

Shannon Barnett, a pediatric psychiatrist at Johns Hopkins Children's Center, says that self-injury blogs do help validate people's feelings, and this is necessary if someone is going to change her or his behavior. However, validation alone is not enough. The process by which teens manage their feelings must be changed in order to stop self-harm, and blogs and chat rooms do not help self-injurers change their thinking processes.[37]

Celebrities Glamorize Self-Injury

The twenty-first century is an age of celebrity. Teens are young, impulsive, and romantic. Mental health professionals who work with self-injuring youth specu-

Do Photographs of Self-Injury Help or Hurt?

Professionals argue that Internet sites that contain images of self-inflicted wounds are harmful because they can trigger the desire to cut in some people. But anecdotal evidence from self-injurers indicates that these sites can be helpful to some people. The photographs that are most likely to trigger self-injurers are close-ups of fresh cuts or scars. A 2008 study asked fifty-two self-injurers to report on whether they found a series of photographs a help or a trigger. The result depended on several factors. Veteran self-injurers found the photos comforting. They felt calmer after viewing the photos and did not feel the desire to self-injure as soon as they usually did. In contrast, people who were new to self-injury said the photos made them want to cut themselves. Also, some people became competitive after viewing the photos. They compared wound sizes and questioned whether some people were *legitimate* self-injurers if their wounds were smaller than those in other photos. Males reported more negative and more competitive views about the photographs than did the females. Some people used the photo archives to get tips on where to cut and how to cut.[c]

late that SI is on the upswing because of the attention given to celebrities who harm themselves. They suggest that when an impressionable young teen learns about a celebrity who has self-harmed, the behavior holds glamour. Celebrity suicides are fourteen times more likely to provoke copycat suicides than when a young person learns of a suicide by a noncelebrity.[38]

Some celebrities, intentionally or not, make self-injury sound like it's no big deal. Christina Ricci reached fame early as Wednesday Adams in the movie *The Adams Family*. In a series of interviews in the late 1990s, she talked about her self-injury. She described putting out cigarettes on her arms as an experiment. She said the pain was an endorphin rush. Ricci told *Rolling Stone* magazine that cutting herself with fingernails or a soda pop top was like having a drink, only quicker. It calmed her.[39]

Other stars exploit self-harm as part of their attempts to entertain the audience. In the summer of 2013, Paris Jackson, the daughter of the pop star Michael Jackson, reportedly slit her wrists after being told she would not be permitted to attend a Marilyn Manson concert. The next night Manson dedicated a song to Paris titled "Disposable Teens." However, this was not a compassionate gesture by the shock rocker. During his performance Manson simulated cutting his wrists. This act was ironic, considering Manson himself has a history of self-injury. However, his entire persona is built on extreme entertainment. He has performed all kinds of bizarre onstage antics, including simulated sex acts, pretending to urinate on stage, and throwing up on stage after he opened a canister of

Celebrity Spotlight: Fiona Apple

Singer-songwriter Fiona Apple has long had a reputation for odd, unpredictable public behavior. She has given tear-streaked interviews and thrown fits on stage when her equipment did not work properly. Her debut album, *Tidal*, was released in 1996 and she won a Grammy award for Best Female Vocal Performance. When Apple took the stage to accept her award, her words were blunt: "What I wanna say is, everybody out there that's watching . . . this world is bullshit and . . . you shouldn't model your life about what you think that we think is cool and what we're wearing and what we're saying and everything. Go with yourself." Some people in the audience loved her directness, others despised her for it.

When Apple was twelve, she was raped in the hallway outside of the apartment where she lived with her mother and sister. This trauma shaped her life. Apple has struggled with an unusual eating disorder. For a time she could not eat foods of certain colors. She said she was not obsessed with her weight. Her goal was to "get rid of the bait that was attached to my body. A lot of it came from the self-loathing . . . I just thought that if you had a body and if you had anything on you that could be grabbed, it would be grabbed. So I did purposely get rid of it."

The first time Apple read a bad review of her music, she scratched her left arm with the nails of her right hand. In a *Rolling Stone* interview she dismissed her self-injury behavior as "I have a little bit of a problem with that. It's a common thing." Sometimes she would bite her lip as hard as she could. When asked if these self-inflicted wounds made her feel better, she said, "It just makes you feel." While Apple insists that she no longer cuts herself with a blade, she still unconsciously scratches her neck while singing or bites her lip until it bleeds.[d]

five hundred dead crickets. Paris Jackson's emotional struggles provided Manson with a ripe opportunity for theater and he seized it.[40]

While there have not been any studies that analyze the influence celebrity self-injury has on a teen audience, young people are impressionable. If they admire someone famous, and that person uses self-harm to cope, it's not a stretch to conclude that the teens might consider this a behavior worth trying. Janis Whitlock of the Cornell Research Program on Self-injury and Recovery calls these high-profile disclosures of self-injury "vectors of social contagion."[41] A vector is a disease carrying organism, like a tick or a flea. Whitlock suspects that celebrity confessions of self-injury spawn destructive behavior in youth in a way that is similar to how watching violent media influences children to behave aggressively. While researchers cannot prove a definitive causal link, there is much data that shows there is a strong relationship between watching violence and acting violently. So while it

Movie Review: Black Swan, Directed by Darren Aronofsky, Fox Searchlight, 2010.

Pressure. Perfection. Performance. Many people who self-injure do so in order to release their inner emotions and anxiety. In the movie *Black Swan*, Natalie Portman masterfully portrays the intense pressure she feels as Nina, a ballerina at the cusp of stardom. Her artistic director pushes her. A rival dancer threatens her. Nina begins to hallucinate. She believes she sees a hangnail on a finger and rips off long strips of her skin. Then she comes back to reality and finds that her finger is fine.

Nina practices dancing for so long that she splits a toenail. Her body has undergone such an aggressive workout that trainers must massage her rib cage and crack her feet and ankles. The movie makes the job of a prima ballerina resemble an ongoing act of self-injury.

Nina loses her grip on reality. She scratches herself in her sleep. During ballet practice she constantly tugs on her back, believing that she is pulling feathers and glass from her skin. Then in the next second, her skin appears to be perfectly normal except for the self-inflicted scratches down her back. The viewer doesn't know which image is real and which is the hallucination, but one thing is perfectly clear: Nina is going crazy. The ending of this movie is tragic and disturbing.

The pressure to perform can cause some people to self-injure in an attempt to calm anxiety.

cannot be argued that celebrity self-harm *causes* teens to hurt themselves, many experts believe that these role models do exert a powerful influence on adolescent behavior.[42]

Social Media Sites Self-Regulate

Because of concern that descriptions and photographs of self-injury might encourage people to harm themselves, social media sites have tightened their posting rules. Tumblr is a site where people can post mini blogs and Instagram is a networking service that lets users take photos and videos and share them on other platforms such as Tumblr and Facebook and Twitter. Tumblr banned self-injury content in February 2012, stipulating that they would not permit any content that glorified or promoted self-injury.[43] Instagram followed suit a few months later, stating in their new guidelines that they wanted to continue to allow people to share their lives with others via images. However, they wanted to grow a "positive and healthy community."[44] Instagram has asked its users to help spot violators by flagging images or content that promotes suicide, eating disorders, or self-harm. These violators will be removed from the site.[45]

However, there is little evidence that this ban is having the desired effect. There are an estimated 197,000 self-harm blogs on the Internet. One study suggested that all the Tumblr ban did was make self-injury bloggers go underground where it makes it harder for advocates to reach people who are suffering.[46] Youth are savvy users of the Internet. They have disguised the content of posts in coded hashtags such as #sue and #secretsociety123. A journalist for the website *BuzzFeed* reported that when she searched Instagram under the hashtag #sue, which is code for suicide, over 800,000 posts came up.[47] The new guidelines of both Instagram and Tumblr depend upon users reporting violations, something that the youth going to these sites are unlikely to do.

Part of the trouble with regulating social media is that people who work with self-injurers do not agree on whether restricting online posts about self-harm is the right approach. Patrick Keohane is a volunteer with ReachOut, an Internet information and support service for young people struggling with mental health issues. He argues that young people of today grew up with technology and are more comfortable asking for help electronically than they are in person. Furthermore, because youth feel so much stigma around mental health, they may not know where or how to ask for help. So banning questions in a forum where people are talking about self-injury may discourage troubled youth from seeking assistance.[48]

The dilemma is how to reduce the possible dangers of the Internet on self-injurers while increasing its potential benefits. Scottye Cash is a professor of social work at Ohio State University. In 2013 she was part of a team of researchers who concluded that teens and young adults use social media sites and mobile devices to communicate thoughts of suicide and to reach out for help. Cash does not think that banning SI posts from social media is the answer. Instead she thinks websites should seize the opportunity to guide troubled teens to sources of assistance. "If something pops up when you search for certain hashtags that can help connect teens to get help in other ways instead of going to a repository of all of the negative things that have been said using that hashtag, that would be a good thing."[49]

In fact, both Tumblr and Instagram currently do just that. People seeking images on Instagram related to self-harm will be redirected to a website called Befrienders.org. It is for a volunteer network dedicated to preventing suicide and self-harm around the world.[50] Liba Rubenstein is a director of public policy at Tumblr. She does not believe that removing content from social media sites solves the problem. In an interview for *BuzzFeed* she stated, "We have the power to take those posts down, but primarily we're focused on the types of intervention," she continued. "Really, our goal is to create dialogue around these behaviors and help people. We want Tumblr to be a place where we facilitate that."[51]

There are other approaches that attempt to harness the power of social media to do good. The National Eating Disorders Association (NEDA) and To Write Love on Her Arms (TWLOHA), an antisuicide group, have amped up their efforts to use social media to promote a healthy message about how to deal with stress. NEDA recruited bloggers from Tumblr to start positive movements on this social media site. For example, *The Love Yourself Challenge* is a Tumblr blog created by a recovering anorexic and her brother. Their site is full of artwork, music links, and inspirational quotes about how to love yourself. NEDA launched its own website Proude2BMe. This is a regulated blog where people can post articles and comments about their struggles with eating disorders, and many of these people also self-harm in other ways too.[52]

Some clinicians believe social media can be a tool to help people with SI. Benjamin Van Vorhees, the head of pediatrics at the University of Illinois' Children's Hospital, began a multimillion dollar study on Internet-based depression intervention. He wants to create a treatment program that combines phone- and Internet-based counseling with a moderated peer-to-peer group. Vorhees believes that such a multifaceted approach might protect at-risk teens from depression before it is even officially diagnosed by a therapist.[53]

With how sophisticated digital technology is today, the phone seems almost old-fashioned. Yet it can be a powerful tool to reach teens and young adults. According to Nancy Lublin, the founder of Crisis Text Line (CTL), the average teen sends and receives close to four thousand text messages a month. Every single one of those messages is opened. Lublin is the CEO of DoSomething.org, an organization that connects teenagers to social action campaigns. Her group found that they were receiving unsolicited messages from youth involved in some of their campaigns. Some of these messages were from teens sounding off about the troubles in their lives. Then one day, Lublin read this message: "He won't stop raping me. He told me not to tell. It's my dad. Are you there?"[54]

This message spurred Lublin and her staff into action. DoSomething.org set up a crisis texting line for teens. CTL is staffed by trained adults and offers teenagers crisis counseling and referrals on a 24/7 basis. Lublin believes texting has great potential to improve lives. She said that research shows teens use texting eleven times more frequently than they do email, and this is not just a technology used by suburban white kids. Even disadvantaged youth today have cell phones, and texting is an integral method of communication. Lublin wanted to establish a program that could help youth like the girl who texted that her father was raping her, but she also wants CTL to harness data that can have broader effects. As she said in a Ted Talk featured on the CTL website, academic studies do not provide enough data on youth behaviors and there are no census reports that provide numbers on how many teens are cutting or are suicidal or are being abused. Lublin makes a strong argument that text crisis hotlines can gather this kind of large sociological data, which could be used to inform legislation and school policies, as well as mental health treatment practices.[55]

Answers and Assistance: TWLOHA

To Write Love on Her Arms is a nonprofit program dedicated to helping people who struggle with depression, addiction, self-injury, and suicide. The founder, Jamie Tworkowski, believes that people were created to love and be loved and that everyone has a story that must be told. In 2006, Tworkowski met a woman who was struggling with self-injury and addiction issues. After she entered a rehab facility, he wrote down her story and titled it "To Write Love on Her Arms." He created a MySpace page where the story was posted and T-shirts were sold to pay for his friend's treatment.

Over time Tworkowski and the others involved realized that this woman's story was the story of many people. The group now raises money through the sale of wrist bands and it uses those funds to run educational and awareness programs about mental health issues. The group also invests their money into treatment programs and operates Storyteller, an awareness campaign designed to encourage high school students to have discussions about mental health issues.[e]

Wrap-Up

Internet blogs and chat rooms. Facebook, Twitter, and Snap Chat. Information spreads digitally from one teen to another with lightning speed. These methods of communication connect people with self-injury disorder, letting them know that they are not alone in their suffering. However, sometimes modern communication can be too raw and too real for young and vulnerable minds. More research needs to be done on the best way to harness the powers of the Internet to help self-injurers find solace and solutions while reducing their exposure to further harm. Young adults need to learn healthy coping mechanisms in order to break the self-injury cycle. This recovery process will be addressed in the next chapter.

THE ROAD TO RECOVERY

If you self-injure, someday you will be discovered. It is just a matter of time. You may choose the time and place to reveal your disorder to others. Or a piece of clothing may slip and reveal a scar. Or your blade may cut too deep and you will be rushed to the hospital. Or one day the ritual of injury no longer works. You hurt more frequently, more severely, but the unwanted emotions do not go away. Or there will come a day when you hate what you do to your body so much that you just want to quit. When this day arrives, it is time to recover.

Detection

Sometimes the self-injurer will be the first to acknowledge how serious her problem is and she will seek help. But more often it is someone close to the person who first realizes that something is wrong. Parents might begin to wonder why

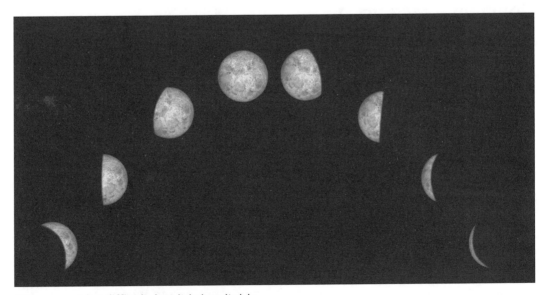

Change can be difficult, but it is inevitable.

their daughter, who used to talk a blue streak, is now silent, does not hang out with friends, and spends hours in her bedroom with the door shut. Friends might glimpse the cuts on an arm in the locker room when the team is changing into their uniforms. A teacher might notice that a student is using a paper clip to gouge a hole into his arm right before a test.

Annie was a junior in high school when her secret was discovered. She had been cutting since her freshman year. Her parents demanded perfection from Annie, and she was bullied in school. When Annie made friends with a girl and saw slash marks on her arm, Annie decided to try cutting too. Finally, she had found something in her life that she could control.[1]

However, one day a teacher noticed a cut on her wrist. The school called her parents and Annie was taken to the hospital. Her mother hovered and worried and pried. Her father characterized Annie's behavior as "teenage bullshit, an attention-getting device."[2]

Annie's parents' reaction is not uncommon. When they discover their child is self-injuring, many parents want to deny that it is happening. They think such a condition only affects crazy people, or they worry that if their child deliberately hurts herself, this must mean they are terrible parents. Worse, in the mind of the parent, is that the self-injury means their child is suicidal. They become afraid to leave their son or daughter alone for a second.

Even relatives and friends who are sympathetic and empathetic still find SI incomprehensible. They just don't get why a person would want to inflict pain on their own bodies. One sister said of her self-injuring sibling, "Why can't you realize everyone has ups and downs, and just deal with life?"[3]

Common Reactions

When parents or friends see scars or bloody clothing, they will understandably panic. Sometimes they will rush you to the emergency room. However, most self-injurers are not suicidal. Fear and panic can actually spawn more fear and panic. The self-injurer is already stressed. If the adults around you panic, your guilt and shame will grow and you may even feel as though your case is hopeless.[4]

You might interpret your parents' panic as anger. Your defenses go up. You withdraw or even act out more. Parents often pry too much or crack down on all freedom after they discover that their child self-injures. You might feel threatened at your loss of independence or suffocated by your parents' constant hovering.

One college student said that after her parents found out that she was a cutter, they hid all the kitchen knives and scissors and any sharp object she could use on her body. This student knew that was a hopeless gesture. "They didn't realize that if you want to cut, you're going to cut."[5] Also, a parent's overreaction can give the self-injurer power. If you know that you can provoke stress in others by harming yourself, you will learn how to use this power to manage your environment rather than learning how to deal with your own internal emotions.

In the essay "Two Sides of Self-Harm," a teen in recovery described the range of typical reactions of people to self-injurers—hands-off or over-involved:

> When someone does self-harm it's usually something that has to do with their mentality in the situation. I can't actually tell someone to stop doing whatever they think helps them. I personally don't think it's a good idea—period. Yet, I can't tell someone that and if I do they won't believe me. . . . Then there's the other side of people who tend to get into others business way too often and feel as though they need to help everyone around them. Those type of people hear that someone has a problem and go to them as soon as they possibly can and ask so many questions.[6]

This young woman used to self-injure, and she knows that no one could make the decision to stop for her. Therefore, she favored the more detached approach. Someone who hovers over the self-injurer is irritating. A college student interviewed for the Cornell Research Program for Self-Injury and Recovery echoed this sentiment. She said when her parents hung around constantly and treated her like a baby, it just sparked her anger. Anger made her want to self-harm.[7]

Realize that when people discover that you self-injure, they might feel disgust or fear. Ideally, they would not reveal these emotions in their body language, but they may. Be prepared. If you are capable of communicating your needs to others when they discover that you self-harm, tell them that you do not need judgment. You need empathy and understanding.

Teen Voice: "Bracelets"

Even if you think that self-injury is your deep, dark secret, someone probably knows. There are signs. One teen poet noticed when her friend began to wear too many bracelets. This behavior was not new. The poet had tried to help her friend before. Now she has grown tired of her friend's lies and secrets, so when the bracelets slip, the poet does not say anything to her friend. But she thinks to herself, "We used to tell each other everything/Now we are separated by the scars you carve on your arm."[a]

Musical Message: "Night and Day" by the Good Life, Album of the Year, Saddle Creek Records, 2004

The album titled *Album of the Year* chronicles a relationship between a guy and a girl. There is one song for each month for an entire year. The single "Night and Day" is a story about discovery and secrets. The lead vocalist, Tim Kasher, sings, "I know a girl with cuts on her legs. I think that she hates the way she was made, but we never spoke of why they were there, I just squeezed them and kissed them 'til we both felt a bit better." The tune is a waltz with an old-fashioned feel highlighted by accordion and electronic piano. These lyrics demonstrate that the scars from self-injury cannot be erased. They track your history in your flesh. It is up to each individual whether to tell the story of how the scars came to be.[b]

Ultimately, no one can stop your self-injury but you. The teen who wrote "Two Sides of Self-Harm" knows that no one else has the right to order her to stop harming herself: "I believe that it's your body, your mind, and you should be able to do whatever you want with it."[8] She knows that self-harm is not an effective coping mechanism, but also recognizes that people need to come to that realization on their own. Are you ready to take that step?

Reasons for Stopping

To someone who doesn't self-injure, the question of whether to stop hurting yourself is a no-brainer. *Of course*, they think. *Why would you want to hurt yourself in the first place?* But giving up self-injury is not so easy for people who have relied on this coping mechanism for years. If you are at this point in your life, it might help to consider why others have chosen to stop self-harming.

Some people stop self-harm because they are finally able to understand how hard it is on the people who love them. That was what Elaine did, a nineteen-year-old who had been a cutter for ten years. One night she violently cut herself. For two hours the bleeding would not stop so she went downstairs. When her parents saw her covered in blood, their reaction seared into her soul. She decided it was time to stop harming herself, not for her own sake, but for theirs. In Elaine's words, "It definitely wasn't me driven; it was other people driven."[9]

If you don't have parents you care deeply about, maybe it's a friend's reaction that will move you. For Mandy it was her best friend. This friend was who she turned to whenever she was deeply troubled. Mandy's best friend talked her through many episodes when Mandy desperately wanted to hurt herself. When her friend told Mandy that if she ever self-injured again, their friendship was over, Mandy decided to quit. "It is not that I'm afraid that she won't speak to me—I'm afraid that if I do it again, it's going to hurt her more. And it's such a private thing to begin with, to have them saying that they'll take care of you, you feel like you owe them so much, it makes them so afraid for you."[10] Mandy's compassion for her friend helped her learn to show some compassion for her own body.

Whether you can truly give up self-injury if you do so for someone else is debatable. Some self-injurers insist that the only way to successfully recover is to change your behavior for yourself, because you really want a different kind of life. Cari, a middle-aged woman, said, "If you stop for others, you're not really stopping, more just postponing. To really stop you have to stop for yourself."[11] That moment when you decide to reclaim your life may not arrive until you have spent a long time self-injuring. A woman named Kim eventually decided that a healthy life was a better life. "I started seeing a benefit with . . . being a good person and being good to other people. People will stop on their own, I think."[12]

Kim had a positive reason for changing her lifestyle. But other people are not so fortunate. Shame and guilt following an act of self-harm can become too much to endure. It was the sight of her many scars that filled Hannah with humiliation. But even the pain of shame can work in a positive way. Hannah said, "Although shame isn't a good emotion, it's been good in the sense that I know that it's not what I need to do anymore."[13]

Sometimes your mortification can be caused by a comment from a family member, but other times a complete stranger's comment can feel like a punch in the gut. That's what happened to Mindy. She was ordering a car wash when the attendant saw her scarred arms. Mindy recalled how the man went on and on about how she was such a pretty girl and how could she do that to herself. She just wanted the guy to leave her alone, and she kept denying that she had cut herself. But then the attendant kneeled down by her car and began to pray for her. He assured her that God would take care of her and promised to pray for her every day. The occasion was momentous for Mindy. "This outside random person is, like, kneeling by my car trying to, like, save me. It was so embarrassing: I felt horrible. I was lying through my teeth to this guy, and he was praying for me. And just, like, he wouldn't stop, he would not stop. That was like a big milestone for me, you know. I think that was a big shift in my act."[14]

When you self-injure, you are doing battle against your own body, and waging war is exhausting. People quit because they are tired. Tired of the secrets. Tired of the hiding. Tired of fighting the urges. Tired of being alone. Just plain tired.

One poster on an Internet forum wrote, "I never thought that in a million years that I would say these words, but I am so tired of fighting my urges to harm. It is so difficult every day to get up and consciously remind myself not to harm, to be careful not to be triggered by someone, not to give into any urges or feelings today. I've got to find a better way."[15] This fatigue sets in with people who have been self-harming for a long time. Not only have they had to physically hide the damage to their bodies, but they have been hiding their emotional selves for years too. Living this secret, double life becomes tedious.

As we age, we grow out of many habits. Self-injury is one behavior that some people are able to just shed like a pair of pants that no longer fit. In her memoir, *Skin Game*, Caroline Kettlewell, describes how her two decades of self-injury ended in fits and starts. She did not experience a great epiphany where suddenly she understood her problem. No single event moved her to stop harming herself. She had more scars than she could count. But she could not even remember the events that triggered most of the scars that marred her skin. So eventually she began to wonder, "Maybe I don't need this anymore. Maybe I never did."[16]

Many people who self-injure quit because they have received professional help. Therapists help them develop better coping skills. Psychiatrists prescribe them medicines that help control their mood swings and impulsivity. These options will be discussed later in this chapter.

 Are You Ready to Stop Hurting Yourself?

Rank these statements from 1 (you completely disagree) to 5 (you completely agree).

1. When I harm my body, I always feel bad about myself shortly afterward.
2. I want to treat my body with more respect.
3. I want to be open and honest when I need help.
4. I want to have a better relationship with the people in my life.
5. I have positive plans for my future.
6. I want to stop using self-injury as a coping mechanism.
7. My future will be better when I stop self-injuring.
8. Self-injury has kept me from doing all that I want so far in life.

Scores of 4 or 5 indicate that you are willing to make changes in your life.[c]

When and how you get to the point where you no longer want to self-injure varies by the individual. So ask yourself some key questions about what you want from life. Then decide. Are you ready to take the next step?

The Process of Recovery

Recovering from self-injury disorder is not like climbing a hill. You will not scramble up to the top and stare in wonder at the beautiful vista of your new life. The experience is more like climbing a mountain range. You climb half-way up, miss your footing, and fall all the way down the mountain. So you begin again. Then you reach a chasm that you are not yet strong enough to cross. So backtrack and try another path. Recovery will not be quick, nor will it be easy. But ultimately, you will reach the summit and a healthier, happier life.

Recovery is a cycle with levels of progression. First, you must become aware that self-injury is not helpful or necessary and you must commit to stop. Secondly, you use coping skills with relative success and you feel optimistic that you will eventually stop all self-injury, despite occasionally backsliding. In the third phase, you have been self-injury free for more than a year, and although you may have urges to self-injure, you do not act on them. How long it takes you to work your way to full recovery depends on several factors. These include the following: whether you have experienced serious trauma such as physical or sexual abuse; the type of support system you currently have; and any accompanying mental health issues you may have, such as borderline personality disorder or an eating disorder.[17]

The case of Robin illustrates the difficulty of the recovery process. She began to self-harm in her early teens years as a way to cope with her father's physical abuse and her mother's suicidal tendencies. When she was in her late twenties, Robin decided to quit self-harm cold turkey. She had stopped drinking that way and assumed she could handle self-injury the same way. She was wrong. To quell her anxiety, Robin overate and overspent. Although she was no longer cutting, Robin still had not developed any healthy means of coping with the stress. Finally, she went to see a therapist. This professional worked with Robin for almost a decade, walking her through the pain of her youth. It took years of hard work and a relationship with someone she trusted before Robin could really say she was recovered.[18]

You have to be the one to decide to give up self-injury. If you try to quit for your parents or your boyfriend or girlfriend or your therapist, you experience short-term success, but the odds of a complete recovery are low. So identify your own reason for why you want to stop harming your body. Keep this reason in the forefront of your mind during the recovery period. And realize that you do not

Celebrity Spotlight: Johnny Depp

Johnny Depp, born in 1963, became a national celebrity with box-office hits such as *Fear and Loathing in Las Vegas* and *Pirates of the Caribbean.* While his talents range from suspense to comedy, he is known for playing eccentric characters such as Edward Scissorhands and Willie Wonka in *Charlie and the Chocolate Factory.* Depp admits to being a bit odd himself. In a 1993 interview with *Details* magazine, he confessed that he was a strange kid: "I used to make weird noises. And I used to do everything twice," such as shutting off the light or circling a telephone pole.

Depp feels emotions strongly, and as a young actor he etched those feelings into his skin. "My body is a journal in a way. It's like what sailors used to do, where every tattoo meant something, a specific time in your life where you make a mark on yourself, whether you do it to yourself with a knife or with a professional tattoo artist." Depp has a series of scars across his left forearm from times he marked himself with a knife. When an interviewer commented that some people might find such an act of self-harm psychotic, Depp's response was classic: "Really? You're not at liberty to judge until after you've eaten that pickled tomato that has been sitting rancid in this deli for months." In his colorful way Depp is saying that we should not judge someone when we have not lived through their struggles.[d]

have to go it alone. There are strategies to help you when something triggers your desire to hurt yourself, and there are trained professionals to guide you through the recovery process.

Assistance from Professionals

Simone was only fifteen years old when her parents brought her to see Dr. Levenkron. He was blunt during their first session. He told her that it would be difficult for them to do the work they needed if she was resistant. Simone asked him what work they needed to do. Dr. Levenkron replied, "The talk between us that will help you stop needing to cut yourself on your arms and legs."[19] Simone was shocked. Self-injury had always been her secret. But Dr. Levenkron gently explained that he would help her use words to express her emotions instead of

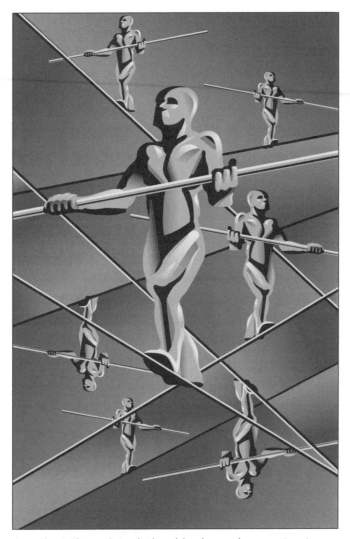

A patient-therapist relationship depends upon trust.

knives. Simone worried that once she had the power to use words, her words might hurt him. Dr. Levenkron insisted that he could choose what power words had over him. If a word hurt too much, he could discard it, and eventually Simone would learn how to do that too. She did stop cutting. Simone was also anorexic and that problem was tougher for her to conquer.[20] But recovery is composed of one small step at a time. Simone found a trusted person to hold her hand when she took that first step.

If you have never worked with a mental health professional before, you might feel intimidated at the thought of how to find someone to help you. Therapists are listed in the yellow pages and online, but who wants to just pick a name randomly and then reveal your most painful secrets to that person? A relationship with a therapist will not work if you don't have trust and if the person is not a qualified professional.

People who self-injure hold on tight to their disorder. Some fear they may die without it, and they are full of shame. It's much safer to keep people at arm's length. Therefore, self-injurers often sabotage their therapeutic relationships. On an intellectual level Simone might have known that Dr. Levenkron was trying to help her. However, on a subconscious level he represented a threat because he would try to convince her to give up the coping mechanism that she believed she would die without. A terrifying thought. You must find a therapist who has experience with patients who self-injure and who is willing to take the time needed to build the trust that is so vital in this relationship.

Seek out someone who is licensed and has expertise with teens and young adults and experience with self-injury patients. There are different types of mental health experts. Psychologists have a doctorate in psychology and are trained in counseling. They should have a PhD as part of their title. Psychiatrists are medical doctors and can prescribe medication. The letters MD should follow their names. Social workers and family therapists have at least a master's degrees and usually work with specific populations such as children, or substance abuse problems and domestic abuse victims.

Try to find a trusted adult to help you find a qualified therapist. Ask a parent or aunt or uncle. If your family's circumstances make that impossible, then go

Movie Review: Prozac Nation, *Directed by Erik Skjoldbjærg, Miramax, 2003*

This movie, based on the memoir of Elizabeth (Lizzie) Wurtzel, dramatically portrays two key aspects of a self-injurer's struggle: the emotional whirlpool that traps people with SI and the nature of a therapeutic relationship that can rescue one from this vortex. Lizzie attends Harvard on a journalism scholarship. She has both a perfectionistic and emotionally needy personality, and before long she plummets into a major depression. Lizzie's form of self-destruction involves lying, casual sex, drugs and alcohol, and one incidence of cutting. Finally, desperate for help as she destroys one relationship after another, Lizzie enters therapy. In her psychiatrist's office, Lizzie can safely reveal her self-loathing and vulnerabilities. Eventually, with the help of her doctor and prescribed medication, Lizzie begins to heal. She described the process of recovery as a slow one. "The same way I went down, I came up. Gradually, and then suddenly."

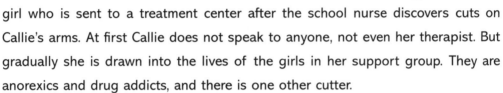

**Read about It: Cut
(New York: Push, 2000)**

The novel *Cut*, by Patricia McCormick, relates the slow recovery of Callie, a fifteen-year-old girl who is sent to a treatment center after the school nurse discovers cuts on Callie's arms. At first Callie does not speak to anyone, not even her therapist. But gradually she is drawn into the lives of the girls in her support group. They are anorexics and drug addicts, and there is one other cutter.

As she begins to recover, Callie silently hands her therapist a piece of metal that she pulled off a cafeteria table. The doctor sets the sharp object on the edge of the desk and says it will stay there until Callie decides what she wants to do with it. Callie is surprised that anyone would give her this much power to harm herself. But the doctor tells her that the world is full of things she could turn into a weapon. Her doctor could not keep Callie safe. She would have to learn how to do that herself.

---

see the school counselor at your high school. If you are a college student, make an appointment with the counseling center on campus. These school professionals are trained in counseling and are a good resource to guide you to further assistance.

Also, insurance companies often have a referral process to help patients find the appropriate help that is covered by their medical plan. If you do not have medical insurance, then call a community health clinic in your area. You can also ask your family doctor to suggest someone. Additionally, most of the organizations listed in the Answers and Assistance sections of this book will aid you in finding appropriate help.

What to Expect from Therapy

There is no easy cure for self-injury. No pill will magically make your desire to self-harm vanish. The disorder has only been defined as a mental illness since 2013, so the mental health profession still has a lot of research to do on treatment. Regardless, there are several treatment options. Be open to trying a variety of approaches with the guidance of your therapist. Your needs will change over time. In the initial stages of recovery what you may most need are strategies to avoid self-harm. Then later on as you stabilize and build trust in your therapist, you will probably be ready to explore some of the complicated emotional issues that underpin your need to hurt yourself. Different techniques work for different people during different times in their lives.

Often, if you are not in a state of immediate crisis, the professional you see will ask you to take some tests or fill out a lengthy questionnaire. Do not be intimidated at the idea of taking a test. It's not like a calculus exam. These psychological instruments are designed to get a lot of information from you in a short period of time. They will aid your therapist in getting a quick assessment of where you might need the most help. The tests are the paper and pencil kind or may just involve the therapist asking you a bunch of questions.[21]

Individual Therapy

Individual therapy is exactly what it sounds like—therapy focused on you, one individual. These sessions will be conversations between you and your therapist. Once you have developed a trusting relationship, you will explore what lies under your self-injury. The key component of individual counseling is to help you sort through your feelings, identify emotional triggers, and interrupt the cycle of self-harm. Therapists have different theories and methods.

Psychodynamic Psychotherapy

Psychodynamic psychotherapy has been around a long time. This type of counseling stems from the theories of Sigmund Freud, the "father of psychology," who was a prominent therapist and scholar in the late nineteenth and early twentieth centuries. Freud believed that dysfunctional behavior stems from unresolved conflicts we had as children that we repress as we age.[22] For example, if a girl was sexually abused by her father as a child, she might not remember the details of the abuse because she locks it in the corner of her brain. However, whenever something jiggles that locked door—a smell, a sound, her father's name—her anxiety, shame, guilt bubble to the surface and she is desperate to make those feelings go away. Therefore, the goal of psychodynamic psychotherapy is to bring our unconscious thoughts to the surface and deal with them so that they no longer haunt us.

Oftentimes in psychodynamic psychotherapy, the patient will transfer some of his or her emotions onto the therapist. This is actually one of the goals of this type of therapy because these feelings can be expressed and examined within a healthy therapeutic relationship. In *Bodies under Siege*, Dr. Armando Favazza discusses several cases of successful treatment through the use of psychodynamic therapy with patients who repetitively and severely self-injured. In particular when the self-injury was related to a major loss in a person's life, such as the death of a parent, researchers found that long-term, regular therapy sessions lessened the need for people to symbolically "kill" their loved one again through damage to their bodies.[23]

Patients who have experienced childhood trauma often need this type of intensive therapy. Psychotherapy is a long-term process during which patients discuss their lives in depth. In essence they relive parts of their past. However, this time they reexperience traumatic events with their therapist by their side. For patients who dissociate, this deep therapy can help them learn how to ground themselves in reality. They learn that they are safe and do not need to mentally vanish to escape a situation like they did when they were a child. They learn to decondition their anxiety as they are exposed to traumatic memories within the safety of the therapist's relationship.[24]

Because psychodynamic psychotherapy is a long-term, intensive process, it works best with older, stable, intelligent patients who can gain insights from the process.[25]

Cognitive Behavior Therapy

Unlike the therapists who believe that self-injury stems from unresolved conflicts in childhood, cognitive behavior therapists maintain that self-injury is a learned behavior. They argue that rather than personality traits or repressed memories of trauma, it is consequences in the environment that determine how we behave. The central belief of cognitive behaviorists is that stressful events do not cause feelings or how the body responds to them. Instead, the way we *choose* to think about stressful events is what causes our feelings. Events lead to perception, which in turn causes emotional and physical responses.

Table 7.1 Behavioral Log

Date	Time	Location	What I See and Hear	What I Think	What I Feel	Positive Action I Took	Results

> **Manage your Impulses**
>
> ● A behavior log or daily diary can help you track your emotional triggers and the actions you take that help you cope without self-harm. Use a form like table 7.1 to record what hurts and helps your recovery process.

Consider the example of two teens who both flunked a math test. One teen realizes that he did not study enough and vows to study harder next time. He is determined and calm. The second teen did not study either, but he starts to obsess that he will fail the semester. He is convinced that the F means he is stupid. He cannot stop worrying. This negative thinking becomes habitual.

In cognitive behavior therapy, patients will learn to identify the emotions that trigger their urge to self-injure, and they develop strategies to prevent them from succumbing to these urges. They learn to replace the negative emotions with positive ones. This type of therapy deals with the symptoms of self-injury, not the underlying causes of what led to the behavior in the first place.[26]

You will practice learning how to assert yourself in individual therapy. Counselors often lead patients in role-playing exercises where they learn how to handle conflicts. For example, Elaine had been anorexic and began to cut as a college student. She did not drink alcohol, and when her sorority sisters teased her for this, Elaine would retreat to her room and self-harm. With the help of her therapist, Elaine practiced what she would say the next time her peers hassled her for not drinking. Elaine practiced until she gained confidence and was able to stand up for herself to her peers.[27]

A specific type of cognitive behavioral therapy is called dialectical behavior therapy, or DBT. It was founded in the late 1980s by Marsha Liehan. It was originally developed to treat suicidal borderline personality disorder patients, but is now used to treat many disorders and has shown success in aiding people who self-injure. DBT is team therapy. A patient attends classes for twenty-four weeks and gets homework in order to learn new, effective behaviors to replace the old, ineffective ones. Patients also have individual therapy once a week throughout the program and access to phone coaching if they experience a crisis. The counselors also receive counseling, an important part of the program as SI is a hard disorder to treat for many therapists because they know their patient is always in danger of harming her- or himself.[28]

DBT is an eclectic therapeutic approach, meaning it uses strategies from different psychological theories. Like behaviorists, DBT practitioners try to recondition patients so they behave differently to stressful stimuli. But DBT also examines the underlying emotions that fuel SI. The primary goal is to stop, or at least reduce the degree and amount of, self-injury and thus improve one's life. DBT practitioners emphasize healthy eating and exercise, and patients are even taught strategies to control their nervous systems when faced with strong emotions. For example, they are directed to hold their breath and dip their faces in a tub of cold water when they feel emotionally overwhelmed. This unusual technique helps patients realize that as the seconds pass, so does the intensity of the emotion, and they learn that they do not need to injure themselves in that particular moment.[29]

Psychopharmacological

Your therapist may prescribe medicine as part of your treatment plan. Many self-injurers have depression and anxiety. Others have trouble turning off their obsessive thoughts. Serotonin selective reuptake inhibitors (known as SSRIs) are a family of antidepressant drugs often used to target these brain patterns. Medication such

What to Expect at Your First Visit with a Therapist

1. Paperwork. You'll have to fill out a lot of insurance forms and questionnaires focused on what you need from the therapist.
2. The therapist will ask why you have sought help.
3. The therapist may ask questions about your family background.
4. Many therapists will require a no-suicide contract at the first visit. This is an on-your-honor agreement designed to help the therapist and your family feel confident that you do not plan to kill yourself. If you have serious suicidal thoughts, then you need to be admitted to a facility to help you through this crisis.
5. The last few minutes of the session, the therapist will summarize his or her understanding of your discussion and you will decide on when you will meet next.

Then the real work begins. You will probably meet on a weekly basis as you explore your past and learn strategies to replace self-injury. Be prepared to feel worse at first. That is a sign that you are recovering.[e]

as Prozac, Paxil, Zoloft, and Celexa are some of the common SSRIs. Each drug has some side effects, but under the right medical supervision they may relieve some of your emotional intensity so that you can focus on developing more effective coping skills.[30] These medicines would be prescribed by a psychiatrist, and you would have periodic meetings with that doctor while you are on the medicine.

Family Therapy

Perhaps you get along well with your therapist. You realize how nice it is to have someone to talk to that you trust. Then one day she brings up the fact that your parents will be joining in on the next session. What?!

Many youth dread family therapy, but it is vital in order to create better communication at home. Often patients are pleasantly surprised to discover that their therapists explore the parents' behavior as much as the patients. But family therapy is not about who is at fault. It is about discovering how family patterns enable youth to self-harm.

Family therapy usually lasts eight to twelve sessions and is very goal oriented. Some of the issues addressed in family therapy include safety, peer relationships, self-harm, and blame. Parents of self-injurers are understandably terrified that their child is going to kill him- or herself. Once they learn that self-injury is a cop-

Family therapy can help rebuild damaged relationships.

ing mechanism and not a suicide attempt, they will also realize that they do not need to spy on their child or tiptoe around him or her. And the youth will learn to verbalize feelings rather than acting on them. The goal in family therapy is to recognize that self-injury is always a choice. Ultimately, the patient is responsible for the damage done to the body. However, parents must also recognize the impact of negative parenting patterns and learn better ways of supporting their child during recovery.[31]

Group Therapy

Self-injury is almost always done in secret. One goal of therapy is to let individuals with common struggles share their experiences. Your counselor may ask you to join a self-injury support group. Being part of these conversations can give you hope and camaraderie and teach you communication skills. Talking with other youth lets you know that you are not alone. They know what the urge to cut feels like. They too have a box of items they use to try to distract themselves when they want to self-harm. They also have days when those distractions just do not work. Your peers will accept you and they will certainly confront you. Often peer relationships are more important to youth than their connections with adults. You may believe that your peers have more credibility because they know what it's like to hurt and bleed like you do.

Group therapy made a difference for Samantha, a sixteen-year-old who had been acting out for the last year. She failed her classes, dated a nineteen-year-old alcoholic, and burned herself. She was sent to group therapy. While she resisted at first, Samantha quickly decided that the girls in her group were "pretty cool." One girl told Samantha that she was going to regret her burn scars when she got older. "They kind of make you look like you have spots," the girl said. Samantha listened and decided to quit burning herself. She stopped cutting school to hang out with the older boy and began to find his constant drinking a turn-off. Samantha slowly gained power over her own life through the aid of her peers.[32]

Self-Help

No treatment program will work if you are not ready to do the hard work of recovery. You need to develop a personal arsenal to use against your despair. If you have a kit of self-injury tools hidden away, it is time to take out that kit and replace it with a recovery tool box. With therapy you will eventually get to the point when you realize that you can survive emotional pain. It will not destroy you. But that realization will take a while. So what alternatives can you use while you are recovering?

Stress Reduction Strategies

Studies have shown that meditation, yoga, and biofeedback have significant physical and mental health benefits. Regular practice can result in decreased depression and anxiety, less physical pain, and a sense of well-being. Biofeedback involves teaching people to control their body's responses. Electrical monitors record your heart rate, pulse, blood pressure, and skin temperature. Patients are provided with electrical scans of these measurements and then practice deep breathing and relaxation to lower their body's stress responses.[33]

Two neuroscientists in Australia believe it is possible to physically alter the neural pathways of self-injurers to change the way their brains operate. Alison, a chronic self-injurer in her twenties, was the guinea pig of the pair of scientists. They measured the electrical activity of Alison's brain prior to her taking an eight-week course on mindfulness meditation, a practice long used by Buddhist monks. Alison's pre-meditation brain scan showed irregularities. She had a lot of activity on the right side of her brain, the side responsible for the emotions of disgust, shame, and sadness. The left side of her brain, the side involved in positive emotions, showed little activity.[34]

Then Alison worked with a mindfulness practitioner. This type of meditation involves a conscious awareness of the present. You learn how to be present with whatever emotion you are experiencing. You do not judge that feeling, just acknowledge it and release it. This is a difficult skill to learn, but the Australian scientists hoped that this practice might help Alison reroute her brain.[35]

After the meditation course ended, Alison returned to the lab for a second brain scan. The activity in her brain had flipped. The right side was now less active, the left side more so. By meditating Alison had created new neural pathways. Mindful meditation is not a quick fix. Alison will have to continue to meditate for the rest of her life to maintain this state of balance.[36] However, this research is an exciting beginning that may lead to more treatment programs for self-injurers. It shows that we are not just the victims of our circumstances or our biology. We can change ourselves from within.

Distractions

When you feel like you need to self-harm, but you do not want to succumb, then you need to get past the urge. Find a way to distract yourself. One idea is to put together a distraction box. It can be an old shoe box or empty tissue container or you can fix up a box to look like something special. It's what is inside this box that matters. Fill this box with items that can help get your mind off the desire to hurt yourself. Then, whenever bad feelings are triggered, go to your distraction box.

Distraction Box

Fill a shoe box with objects that distract you and a list of activities you can try the next time you have to urge to injure. Keep track of what works so you can use these techniques again.

Activity List

- Go to park and swing
- Journal/write poetry
- Draw/paint what you feel inside
- Masturbate
- Sing loudly
- Play with a child or a pet
- Breathe deeply
- Be with friends
- Rip paper into thin shreds
- Last resort—take red pen and mark arms like you would if cutting

Objects to Put in the Distraction Box

- A funny, uplifting movie
- Lucky charms or crystals
- Crochet hook and yarn so you can make a scarf
- A rubber ball to squeeze
- A photograph of someone you love
- A list of people you can call
- A CD of music that soothes you

Remember that self-injury is a choice. You have the power to a select a positive alternative to self-harm.

Tell People How You Feel

In order to recover, you will have to take on new responsibilities. Verbalize your feelings before you hurt yourself. If you learn to talk about your pain, you will be less likely to want to cause yourself physical pain. Learn to identify the feelings that are associated with your desire to harm yourself. Break down these emotions into small components. What is really bothering you?

Tony was a tall, thin fifteen-year-old with a severe case of acne. He could not tell his therapist exactly what bothered him. In Tony's words, his life sucked. His doctor pushed him: "What exactly sucked?" Through careful questioning by the therapist and deeper thinking on Tony's part, he finally admitted that what really bothered him was his acne. He felt destined to have bad skin forever. His therapist gave Tony suggestions about seeking help from a dermatologist. He began to feel a glimmer of power and hope instead of an overwhelming sense of despair.[37] If you break down your emotions into small components, it is easier to problem-solve solutions.

You must also learn what triggers your urge to self-harm. If you are aware of your triggers, you can predict and be prepared when a situation arises. Part of dealing with those triggers is verbally communicating with friends, family, school personnel, and other adults. If you feel hurt, angry, or rejected, withdrawal is not the answer. Communicate your feelings and then if you still do not get your needs

Teen Voice: the Future Speaks

This anonymous post in a self-injury forum reveals one person's regret. "I hate them [scars]. They're embarrassing and they remind me of horrible times in my life. I never have that "I survived" feeling when I see them. It just makes me really sad to look at them." If you feel the urge to self-injure, pause and think of what your future self would say to your current self. Look forward. Think hard about how your future will be impacted if you continue to self-injure. Not only the scars your body will show, but also if you do not learn how to cope with life's stressors now, then how will you manage as a spouse, an employee, a parent. Now is the time to reclaim your life.[f]

met, readjust. Maybe you need to make new friends or stop looking to that family member for kindness. You cannot control other people's behavior. But you can be the driver of your own life and stop giving other people power over how you feel.

In addition to thinking about how you communicate to others, think about your own self-talk. Are you kind to yourself? Do you put yourself down? Would you want to be friends with you? Treat yourself the way you would treat your best friend. Work to make the inside of your head a comfortable place to be.

A Safe Space

One strategy that helps self-injurers is to create a safe space. This could be a real place or a completely fictitious spot. Imagine a safe place where you would feel

Practice visualizing a safe place to which you can mentally escape when life gets stressful.

Answers and Assistance

LifeSIGNS is an informational and support network from the United Kingdom. It was created in 2002 to help self-injurers find new ways to cope with emotional pain. The organization is led by volunteers. The LifeSIGNS website has many links to fact sheets about self-injury as well as suggestions for healthy ways to manage stress. Additionally, there is information for friends and family of people who self-injure. LifeSIGNS also operates a supportive forum that focuses on recovery.[9]

calm. A shaded forest path. A stretch of deserted beach. A walk-in closet with a comfy chair, a favorite quilt, and music in the background. In the arms of someone you love. List the things you'd put in this place. Can you create this space right now?

You will not always be able to get to your safe space when you feel stressed. Use imagery to create so you can always carry it with you in your mind. What does this place look like, feel like, smell like, sound like, and taste like? When you have the urge to self-injure, close your eyes, breathe deeply, and in your mind go to this place until you feel calmer.

Wrap-Up

The chances are high that one day someone will discover that you self-injure. They will probably be shocked. Maybe even revolted. And definitely they will be afraid for your safety. These are common responses.

While it is natural to worry about how other people think about your self-injury disorder, the most important opinion is your own. When you decide to take the first step to recovery, no one can take that decision away from you. The process of healing will be slow, and painful, with many backward steps, but with the benefit of trusted, competent mental health professionals, a network of support, and love for yourself, you will succeed.

FOR FRIENDS
AND FAMILY

If you are reading this book and do not have SI yourself, I'll bet you know someone who does. Is it your son or your daughter? Your best friend or maybe one of your students?

You must be frightened by the thought that this person you care about deliberately wounds his body. You're probably revolted by the idea too. And angry. After all, doesn't he know that you care about him? Doesn't he realize that you would do anything to take away his pain?

Maybe or maybe not.

But you see, your feelings are not the issue here. The self-injurer's feelings are the ones that matter most. People hurt themselves because they know of no other surefire way to rid themselves of the emotional pain that threatens to engulf them. But you should know this already if you have read the earlier chapters in this book that explained why people harm themselves. If you haven't read these chapters, then do it now.

Yes, right now before you continue reading this chapter.

You will not be any help to your loved one unless you understand who she is and why she chooses to damage her body. When you are done reading, come back to this page because this chapter is for you.

Yes, you are afraid and hurt and disgusted and angry, and you have a complete right to feel all of those things. This chapter will attempt to answer your questions about self-injury and help you determine how best to help your loved one recover.

Signs of Self-Injury

So you suspect that someone you care about is self-injuring, but do not know for certain? Here is a list of signs that an individual may be harming him- or herself.

- Unexplained scars, cuts, or burns
- Wearing long-sleeves and long pants even in warm weather
- Refusing to participate in activities that require exposure of the body such as gym class or swimming
- Constant wearing of wrist bands or extensive bracelets
- Possession of unusual paraphernalia such as razor blades or an X-Acto knife
- Unbelievable explanation for repeated injuries such as getting scratched by a kitten
- Seeming physically or emotionally absent or distant
- Seeming overwhelmed by daily activities such as work or school
- Having an eating disorder or abusing drugs or alcohol
- Depression or anxiety

Have you seen some of these signs in a person close to you? If so, it is possible that he or she is engaging in acts of self-harm. You are doing the right thing by reading this book. Educate yourself on SI so you can understand the struggles your loved one is going through. Read the books and novels, watch the documentaries, and contact the organizations identified throughout these chapters. Knowledge is power, and in the battle against self-injury disorder, it is one of the only elements of power that you will be able to exert.

Movie Review: The Silent Epidemic, Directed by Ili Bare, Beyond Productions, 2010

Self-injury is a global problem, and much of the research on treatment is led by scientists in Europe, Canada, and Australia. In 2008, Professor Graham Martin conducted the Australian National Epidemiological Study of Self-Injury. A sample of twelve thousand people was interviewed, and the data revealed that about 8 percent of the Australian population self-injured over the course of their lifetime. The 2010 documentary *The Silent Epidemic* follows three of these individuals and the mental health experts who are trying to treat them. This film is not just another science documentary. The narrative is a blend of cutting-edge research and personal stories. Ultimately, *The Silent Epidemic* is the story of self-harm, science, and optimism.

Q & A for Family and Friends

I bet you feel powerless, way out of your league. There is no parent class or best friend class on what to do when you believe someone close to you is deliberately carving or breaking or burning their body. No university has a class titled Self-Injury 101 for educators or coaches. This section will address some common questions that family and friends have about self-injury.

What Should I Say or Do?

One thing is for certain—do not just ignore the situation. Self-injury will not just go away if you pretend it isn't happening. And try not to show extreme shock or disgust. Your first reaction might be to call the self-injurer crazy. That will not help. Remember, the person with SI does not view her behavior the same way as you do. While to you the behavior seems repulsive and horrific, she is positive that it is key to her survival.

Experts in the field offer a couple responses that a friend or parent can say to their loved one. Lori Plante, the author of *Bleeding to Ease the Pain*, suggests you recite this simple sentence to the self-injurer: "This [injury] really tells me how badly you're hurting. I'm glad that you've told me and I'm committed to helping

---

Musical Message: "Because of You" by Nickleback, The Long Road, Roadrunner Records, 2003

"Because of You" is a pounding, painful rant sung by Nickleback, a Canadian rock band that was formed in the mid-1990s. The lyrics reveal the pain that SI causes the people who care for the one who self-harms. This is no ballad. The drum beats in rapid frustration to an angry sounding guitar. "Hands on the mirror, can't get much clearer," cries lead singer Chad Kroeger. "Now that you're bleeding, you stare at the ceiling and watch as it all fades away." The singer has sworn that he won't come each time the self-injurer calls, but he cannot help himself. He comes, but resents it. This song could be about a suicide attempt or it could be about self-injury. One thing is for certain: the song represents the absolute powerlessness friends and family feel when someone close to them continues to self-harm.[a]

you get through it in your own way."[1] This response acknowledges the person's self-injury, but also recognizes that he or she is ultimately the one in control of what comes next.

Karen Conterio and Wendy Lader, authors of *Bodily Harm* and cofounders of S.A.F.E. Alternatives, offer this simple response: "I've been terribly concerned about you. I see all these scars on your arms, and I suspect you may be hurting yourself. If that's the case, I want you to know that you can talk to me about it. I just want to help. . . . If you can't talk to me, please talk to somebody else."[2]

How Do I Get Him (or Her) to Talk about It?

If someone who self-injures could verbalize his emotional pain, he probably would not need to harm himself. The thought of putting emotions into words is terrifying and impossible for many self-injurers. Asking him to tell you why he hurt himself might put up a wall between you. It is very possible that the self-injurer does not know why.

Instead tell him that you understand that this must be a really hard thing to talk about. That simple statement establishes your empathy. Maybe that is all you need to do at first, in addition to being there as silent support for this person. Strong and safe attachments to friends and family are the most important resources a young person can have. Teens often communicate what they need belligerently and confusingly, and it is easy to overreact. Annie's father's hostile response was described in chapter 7. He thought Annie had self-injured just to get attention, and it made him furious. Annie's mother had an opposite, but just as extreme, reaction. She hovered and questioned, wanting to know details of Annie's sessions with her therapist. "She wanted to know why I was feeling this way," Annie said. "But by this point I wouldn't allow myself to tell her anything. Three years of secrecy, pain, hiding—the gulf was too big. I felt guilty, though, because my mother did care, cared too much, was constantly worried. So that was another reason I didn't tell her. I wanted to protect her, to shield her from what was going on inside me."[3]

Despite your own anger and fear, give your loved one time to learn how to express herself verbally and how to have a real discussion instead of the two of you communicating past each other. Young self-injurers need to learn empathy which is a skill that can be learned. At first, their pain is the only thing that exists. But therapy can help them learn to see events from the point of view of others. Most people who self-injure are super sensitive. Perceived rejections balloon in importance in their minds and they seek quick relief from that emotional pain through self-injury. Many therapists will role-play with their patients. In this safe setting, the youths can practice expressing their pain and

Celebrity Spotlight: Troian Bellisario

Troian Bellisario is the lead character, Spencer Hastings, on the ABC drama *Pretty Little Liars*. In January 2014, she spoke out about her history of self-harm in an interview on *Good Morning America*. As a teenager Bellisario struggled to fit into the mold of what others wanted her to be. The actress said that she "went down a very, very dangerous path and I honestly believe I wouldn't be here today if it weren't for a number of incredible people, friends and family." Bellisario's self-harm began as a junior in high school. She did not eat and she cut herself. The downward spiral stopped when her parents read her journal and then staged an intervention. This led to Bellisario, for the first time ever, telling her parents about the blackness and darkness and rage inside of her, some of it directed at them. The actress acknowledges that recovery is a day-to-day process. "Sometimes I feel like I'm trying too hard, like I don't belong." But when a sense of failure or inadequacy creeps up on her, Bellisario knows who to turn to. "My friends and my family—the people who I love and who love me back. Whenever I get down, when I want to crawl under a rock, I just look around at them and I see how rich my life is."[b]

anger and love and can learn how to listen as well.[4] So be patient. Do not pressure your loved one to talk.

How Do I Get My Loved One to Stop This Self-Harm?

You can't. Those are hard words to read, but it is true. You cannot control whether the person you care about self-injures. The only person you can control is yourself. However, you have the perfect right to establish boundaries for yourself. Mandy's experience was discussed in chapter 7. She decided to stop harming herself when her best friend said she would no longer be her friend if Mandy injured again. Before you take a step like this one, clearly explain why you can no longer be in a relationship with a person who self-injures and help the person find assistance and alternatives to self-harm.

Of course, if you are a parent you cannot so easily cut off ties with your child when he or she self-injures. And issuing ultimatums, supervising around the clock, and removing all sharp objects from your house are not going to solve the

Twelve-Step Programs

Many people are familiar with Alcoholics Anonymous, the original twelve-step program started in 1935 when Bill Wilson, an alcoholic, met with Bob Smith, another drunk, in an attempt to stay sober. Their idea was that talking to another person who was going through a similar addictive struggle would help them remain sober—one day at a time. The experience of these two men spawned an international movement that today has offshoot groups for people struggling with addictions ranging from alcohol and drugs to gambling and sex, and there are groups for family members of these addicts as well.

Twelve-step programs have twelve guiding principles that are essentially guidelines for right living. You take an inventory of your life, try to make amends for past wrongs and recognize that you ultimately do not have control over what happens in your life. You turn over that control to a higher power. For some people this higher power is a religious entity, but for others it might be nature or fate. You do not have to be religious to attend a twelve-step program.[c]

problem. It might make it worse as the two of you will probably get into power struggles. Instead, insist that your child get help from a qualified therapist and seek help for yourself. At present there are limited options available specifically for families of people who have SI. However, because this disorder has addictive properties, many people find that twelve-step programs can be helpful. These are community-based, peers-helping-peers groups. No therapist is present. People with family members who struggle with addictive behaviors come together to listen to each other's stories without judgment.[5] There are twelve-step programs for many addictions, although not yet for SI. However, one group is called Families Anonymous. This is a program for parents and grandparents concerned about addictive behaviors in their children, even adult children. Another twelve-step program is Co-Dependents Anonymous, or CoDa. This group recognizes that often addiction is a family disease. The parents and siblings and significant others of self-injurers have played a role in maintaining this behavior. CoDa is for people who want to work on developing healthy, functioning relationships.[6]

What If My Loved One Refuses to Acknowledge That SI Is a Problem?

If you are a parent and your child is a minor, it is your responsibility to get her the psychological and medical help she needs. She may fight you, but you need to exert the control to get professional assistance. If she argues that her SI is no big problem, you can say, *OK, if it's not, then the expert will tell me that you do not need further mental health assistance.* Try explaining that her self-injury frightens you and you really need someone with professional expertise to tell you whether this behavior is serious or not. Keep it a low-pressure exchange.

It may also help if you give your child some choices about where to seek assistance. In the book *Bodily Harm*, the cofounders of S.A.F.E. Alternatives treatment program shared that a teen who found her way to their facility had been given three treatment options by her parents.[7] No one likes to be controlled by others, especially teenagers. Choices give them a sense of agency so they do not feel as though they are going to lose all power over their own lives.

If your loved one is an adult, then the situation is more complicated. If she is actively suicidal or homicidal, she can be committed to a treatment center against her will. But if she is not, then all you can do is decide on what terms you will continue your relationship with this person. Karen Conterio and Wendy Lader of S.A.F.E. Alternatives recommend that you do your best to let the self-injurer know that she is not the only person who is impacted by SI. They have found that when people realize how much those around them suffer when they self-harm, their resistance to treatment crumbles.[8]

What Should I Tell Other Family Members about My Loved One's SI?

That depends on how old they are and what their direct relationship with the self-injurer is. If you have young children in your family, they may not have the developmental skills to understand the complicated nature of SI. Talk with a therapist to find an effective way to let small children know what is happening, if that is even necessary. Let them know that the self-injurer loves them and she is working on her problems, which have nothing to do with them. And encourage them to talk to you if they have questions or worries about what is going on.

With extended family members you have to be careful not to get defensive if they show negative reactions toward your loved one who is self-injuring. Remember that the most common reaction of people to SI is fear and revulsion. Although the public has more awareness of SI today than it did even a decade ago, much stigma remains. But you do not have to explain everything. You can turn over at least some of that responsibility to the self-injurer. Dealing with other people's reactions is a natural consequence of the choice she makes to self-harm.

Is It My Fault That My Loved One Self-Injures?

No. Self-injury is always a choice. The disorder may have addictive properties. Your loved one may have experienced childhood trauma. She or he may struggle with other mental illnesses. Despite these realities, the person ultimately responsible is the individual who chooses self-injury over other types of coping mechanisms.

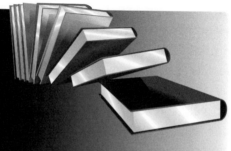

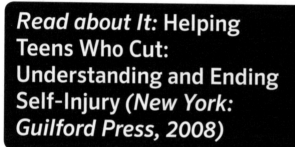

Read about It: Helping Teens Who Cut: Understanding and Ending Self-Injury *(New York: Guilford Press, 2008)*

Michael Hollander is an expert in the field of SI. He has worked with teens and their families for three decades. This book is part informational guide, part workbook. In clear language, Hollander explains why young people self-injure and how to help them recover. His entire focus in this book is family members, specifically parents. Each chapter is full of anecdotes that illuminate examples of effective and ineffective ways of communicating with your child. His advice is blunt and practical. For example, one of his key pieces of advice to parents is to be patient. This advice is immediately followed by what he anticipates would be the natural response from a parent: "You want me to be patient while my child is self-injuring? You can't be serious! Doctor, slip into your pajamas because you must be dreaming."[d]

But Hollander shoots right back with what he knows from decades of experience is the reality of self-injury. "Well, you do have a choice: you can either be impatient with your child and yourself, suffer, and make the situation worse, or you can find a way to be patient, and in all probability, more helpful."[e] No-nonsense advice given in a no-nonsense style. This book would be a helpful reference for anyone who cares about someone who self-injures.

Given that, you are in a relationship with this individual. If you are the parent of the self-injurer, you have been a factor in how she or he has developed. It is important to acknowledge that. The dynamics of families are complicated. Do not minimize or dismiss how you may have contributed to your loved one's condition. Be open to understanding the part you have played.

This recognition is not about blame. It is about growth. Do not punish yourself for bad decisions you might have made earlier in life. Instead, learn to grow and change alongside of your loved one who is trying to heal.

What Do I Do with My Own Strong Emotions?

What you are going through is hard. When you first discovered that your loved one self-injured, you were probably shocked. However, you cannot deny the behavior. If you do not acknowledge the self-injury, you are not admitting how much emotional pain your loved one is in.

Shock may have been followed by anger. One parent interview by researchers with the Cornell Research Program on Self-injury and Recovery said, "There is a frustration in terms of that little voice in the back of your mind that is saying 'just stop it!' It's very hard, I think knowing more about the condition and about the underlying factors makes it easier to push that little voice away."[9] Frustration is hard to deal with, but remember that what seems simple to you is not so easy for your loved one. And you cannot control the self-injury behavior, so your anger, while understandable, is not helpful.

Sadness and sympathy and empathy all show how much you care about your loved one. However, they can also come across in a condescending way. Your loved one does not need pity. She needs understanding and patience and support.

Guilt—as natural a part of parenting as changing diapers and driving kids to sports practice. It is natural to feel guilty about what you did or did not do in the past. However, you must remind yourself, as was stated earlier in this chapter, that your behavior may have played a part in your loved one's development, but you did not cause her to self-injure.

So what are you supposed to do with all these emotions brewing around inside you? Take care of yourself using the same kind of stress-reduction techniques you hope your loved one will learn. Consider the things you already do when you feel stressed: work out, call a friend, eat a pint of ice cream, have a drink, go for a walk, meditate. Some of these strategies may be healthy and some may not be. During this very stressful time of life, when someone you care about is struggling to recover from self-harm, perhaps it is time to add some strategies to your coping tool kit. Consider a yoga or meditation class. Perhaps you can find relief in a creative outlet such as music or a painting class. Exercise is a surefire way to release

Meditation can be a tool to help manage stressful emotions.

stress and has many physical benefits. And don't rule out therapy for yourself. You need someone outside of your family to talk to, your own support system.

Maybe you think you're doing just fine. You have discovered that your loved one self-harms, but you have been through worse troubles in your life. You can deal with this.

Do yourself a favor. Run through the list on table 8.1 to gauge whether you are coping as well as you think. Sometimes our bodies send out signs that our brains refuse to acknowledge.

If you recognize some of these signs in yourself, it is time to implement some stress-reduction strategies.

Table 8.1 Signs of Stress

Do You Feel This Way?	Do You Think This Way?	Do You Act This Way?	Has Your Body Changed in This Way?
You feel nervous for no reason.	You think bad thoughts about yourself.	You cry for what seems like no reason.	Your muscles are always tensed.
You feel crabby all the time.	You cannot concentrate on your school work.	You act without thinking.	Your hands are cold or sweaty.
You feel afraid when there seems to be nothing to fear.	You forget simple things.	You laugh nervously.	Your back and neck hurt.
Sometimes you feel like you are on the verge of panic.	Your mind is stuck on the same thought over and over.	You argue easily.	You can't fall asleep or can't stay asleep.
	You worry about failing.	You try risky behaviors, like smoking or drinking alcohol or using other drugs or experimenting sexually.	Your stomach feels queasy a lot.
	You don't have any fun anymore doing things you used to enjoy.	You have no appetite.	You're tired all the time.
		You eat a lot of comfort food.	Your heart races.
			Your head aches.
			Your mouth is dry.
			You constantly have a head cold.
			Your jaw aches from clenching it so hard.
			You have difficulty swallowing.

Sources: D. Ballesteros and J. L. Whitlock, "Coping: Stress Management Strategies," the Fact Sheet Series, Cornell Research Program on Self-Injury and Recovery, Cornell University, 2009, http://www.selfinjury.bctr.cornell.edu/perch/resources/coping-stress-management-english-1.pdf (accessed December 21, 2014); "Stress Test," *Psychologist World*, http://www.psychologistworld.com/stress/stresstest.php (accessed January 25, 2015).

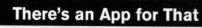

There's an App for That

Meditation has potential to help self-injurers. Chapter 7 discusses recent research on the benefits of mindfulness training. However, it is not just people with SI who need to learn how to manage stressful emotions. We all do. Headspace is an online resource and mobile app service created by Andi Puddicombe. After four friends died in one year, Puddicombe went on a search to learn more about meditation. He trained under the Dalai Lama and became a Buddhist monk. Then at age thirty-two, he created Headspace, a mobile app with ten-minute meditation programs. While there is a cost for this app, you can try the program for free for ten days.

The goal of mediation is to incorporate Zen into your life. Zen is a combination of relaxation and focus. With practice, you can learn how to acknowledge your emotions without being ruled by them and have a more fulfilling life.[f]

How Do I Handle a Power Struggle?

Power struggles with teenagers and young adults are inevitable. It is part of the developmental process that young people are experiencing in these critical years of their lives. However, when you have a youth who self-injures, these power struggles take on a new intensity. If your child self-harms, you are probably terrified that if you get into an argument with her or punish her, she will retreat to her room and hurt herself.

The best way to deal with power struggles with your teen is to avoid them. Often these arguments are more about control than they are about a particular request the teen makes of the parent or vice versa. So when you feel the intensity of the situation begin to mount, disengage from the situation. If your child wants to vent, let her. You should not ignore her, but you can calmly (at least outwardly calmly) say that you will listen to her, consider what she is saying, and address it later, after you have time to reflect on her points. Your child cannot get into an argument if there is no one to argue with. So listen, but do not verbally participate.[10]

No one likes to lose. Try to create an outcome in which both you and your teen walk away with something you want. As you reflect on the issues your child raised, decide what a nonnegotiable issue is for you. Say your child wants to go to the mall with a friend who been a source of conflict for your daughter before.

over what is a terrifying disorder. No-harm contracts also set up clear behavioral expectations that may help youth manage their impulses to injures themselves. Finally, the very word *contract* communicates how serious SI is. Some people believe that establishing these clear-cut expectations with youth helps to let them know that they are responsible for the choices they make.[12]

However, not everyone agrees that the benefits of no-harm contracts outweigh the negatives. If you pressure your child into signing such a contract, then this document can become part of a power struggle between the two of you. In addition, because the contract forbids self-harm, that is where the focus is—on the self-injurious behavior. While that dangerous behavior is definitely important, what really matters for your youth is to get at the underlying emotional needs that pressure him to hurt himself. So the contract might unintentionally shift attention from where it needs to be. And, let's be realistic, your child is probably going to slip up. Recovery is a process of taking one step forward and two steps back. So a self-harm contract is setting up your child to fail.[13] No one feels good when they fail. And for a self-injury, feeling bad is a very bad thing. Work closely with a therapist to decide if a no-harm contract is the best approach to take with your loved one.

Wrap-Up

You probably have many other questions about SI. This book is just a starting point if someone you care about has this disorder. Know that you are not alone. Millions of parents, siblings, friends, and colleagues struggle to know the right thing to do or say when they believe that people in their lives are hurting themselves

Answers and Assistance:
National Mental Health Association

Mental Health America has been working in communities to aid the mentally ill for over a century. Their role is to educate the public, advocate for improved mental health policies, and provide important services to mentally ill people and their families. Visit their website at http://www.mentalhealthamerica .net/. It is a good place to access resources, including referral information to help you find a qualified professional who can aid your family through recovery.

intentionally. Your feelings of fear and anger and guilt are normal and under-standable. Do not let remorse or shame cripple you. Like any illness, SI does not just affect the person who is afflicted with it. The disorder permeates everyone whom that person encounters. Therefore, you must take care of yourself. Work on your own stress reduction methods. Seek out someone that you can talk to so that you do not carry the burden of your loved one's self-injury alone.

RAISING AWARENESS— TELL YOUR STORY

W hen you have stopped self-injuring, you should feel proud. You have a tool-box of healthy ways to cope with stress. You understand your emotions and have come to terms with traumas in your past. But now you face new challenges: What do you tell people about your history of self-harm? What will you do if you suspect someone else is self-injuring? What role will you play in changing the national dialogue about self-injury disorder?

Coming Out

As you contemplate whether or not to tell your story to someone, ask yourself these questions: Where are you in your recovery? Have you spent enough time thinking about why you self-injured? Do you understand your actions clearly enough to explain them to someone else? How strong is your ego? If people respond to your scars with fear and disgust, are you strong enough to handle it?

Think deeply about why you want to tell a particular person about your self-harm. Will it help you get closer to him or her? Will confessing help you be more honest with yourself? Be confident of your purpose in revealing your self-injury before you take that step. If you clearly understand what your goal is in revealing this secret, you are more likely to get what it is that you seek.

If you decide to tell someone about your disorder, make a plan. Pick the correct time and place and method. It can be empowering to reveal your secret self-injury face-to-face and this method also allows you to read the other person's body language. However, communicating via email or a letter allows you to say what you want to say without interruption. This was the method a woman identified as C chose to tell her best friend. She shared her story on the website LifeSIGNS.

I told my best friend first. I'm extremely nervous when it comes to talking, so instead I wrote it down and then she could read it. I was worried that

Revealing that you have self-injured through a letter lets you communicate without interruption.

she'd think differently of me, that it would change our friendship, maybe that she wouldn't want to be friends with me. . . . When I later told my other best friends, I was worried about how they'd react. Some were a bit shocked; another actually came out herself, because I had. I thought they might not like me anymore, or think there was something wrong with me. But they've all been really good.[1]

This woman said that although it was difficult, coming out to her friends was the best thing she could have done because now when she feels the desire to self-harm, she has people to talk to instead of being so alone.

If you choose to come out in person, make sure you pick an occasion when you and your listener are not in a hurry. This could be a long and complicated conversation. Also, be sure that you are both calm before you begin. Do not reveal your history of self-injury during an argument.

A Script

If you would rather reveal your SI in a letter than face-to-face, here are some sentence starters.

Dear _____,

   I'm going to tell you something and I don't want you to freak out. If you freak out, that's not going to help me at all. I have a secret. Sometimes when I feel _____. I hurt myself by _____. The reason I hurt myself is because it helps me _____ _____. I wanted to tell you about this because _____ _____. The best thing you can do to help me is _____ _____.

                                        Love,
                                        Me

Then, when you are ready, keep it simple. Tell the person that sometimes you hurt yourself as a way to cope when you're feeling bad. Your listener will probably be shocked. Certainly, he or she will have questions; will probably want to know why you hurt yourself. Try to explain, in general, the things that trigger you, such as pressure, anxiety, or depression. But do not go into detail about your methods of self-injury or show your scars. Keep the focus on the emotional issues involved in your disorder. Also, remember that you do not have to cover everything in this first discussion. Do what is comfortable for you.

Of course, you hope that anyone you come out to will be supportive and understanding, but be prepared for less positive reactions. Self-injury is a very disturbing concept for most people. You may encounter fear, anger, and disgust.

That was the reaction Ravyn received from some of her friends when she accidently came out. This high school student was distracted one day and took off her jacket when she was sitting with a group of friends. Ravyn was only wearing a tank top and her scars shocked the people around her.

It was fairly obvious I had done it myself. To start with I got a huge hug off of one of my friends. She was so helpful and lovely to me through the

Celebrity Spotlight: Demi Lovato

Singer and actress Demi Lovato looks like a woman who has it all. Talent, beauty, success. But she has struggled for years. As a girl, Lovato was frequently teased about her weight. As a result, she developed an eating disorder and depression, which eventually morphed into self-injury. The first time Lovato cut herself she was only eleven years old. She said she was trying to make the outside match the pain she felt on the inside.[a]

Eventually, Lovato checked into a treatment center where she was diagnosed with bipolar disorder. She remained at the facility for three long months. Thoughts of her little sister helped her through the darkest days of treatment. Lovato knows that because she is a celebrity, young people look at her as a role model, and therefore, she chose to speak out about the emotional difficulties she has faced. "If I can prevent one person today . . . from cutting for the first time . . . I can . . . change one life by saying don't go there."[b]

After you reveal that you self-harm, people might react negatively.

whole experience and the year ahead. Then one of my friends took me to the side, she looked so upset, she told me that I shouldn't do it and I should stop. But the person who was supposed to be my "best friend" did something I still don't understand. . . . After that it got all around school and people walked past me in the corridors mimicking slicing up their arms. They looked at me as if I was something nasty on the bottom of their shoe.[2]

Be prepared for the people you tell to withdraw from you, at least for a while. Give them time to recover from the shock of what you have revealed. Consider giving your friends and family this book or recommending some of the resources in these pages. Learning more about self-harm will help them better understand what you have been going through.

Then, regardless of what the reaction is of your listener, be proud of yourself for revealing this painful fact about your past. Telling your story is a sign that you are healing.[3]

Scars

Unlike other disorders, self-injury leaves scars. Even if you cover them with clothing or tattoos, you will know they are there. Elaine was afraid to tell her first boyfriend about her scars. She no longer self-injured, but she was afraid that when he saw them, he would dump her.[4] Elaine's fears are normal. Former self-injurers often regret what they have done to their bodies. They look back on their old patterns of behavior and wonder how they ever could have been so crazy.

But for some people scars are not a completely negative reminder of their past. They can focus your recovery. One cutter named Bree said that looking at her scars reminded her of a time in her life that she does not want to return to. "When I see the words I've written on my body—DIE or PAIN or HATE—it reminds me to do my maintenance, the things I have to do every day to keep serenity in my life."[5]

One day someone might catch you off guard by commenting on your scars. One woman who had been self-injury free for seven years posted online about an incident that happened to her when she was hanging out with a group of friends who knew nothing about her disorder. One of the guys noticed a scar on her arm and asked how she got it. The woman lied and said she fell while she was mountain biking. Then another friend said, "Oh, she's just a cutter." The woman became flustered, worried that this friend had discovered her secret past. Then she realized that he was joking.[6]

In a self-injury chat room, the woman asked how other people handled these off-the-cuff comments. One person replied that when she was working in a cof-

Musical Message: "Warrior" by Demi Lovato, Demi, Hollywood Records, 2013

The last song on Demi Lovato's fourth album is titled "Warrior," and it is a confessional. She sings about her 2011 breakdown during which she was diagnosed with bipolar disorder, and reveals that she was bulimic and injured herself to cope with emotional stress. Desperate to get this story off her chest, Lovato found the song simultaneously easy and excruciating to write. It was easy because she wanted to tell her story and let go of the painful experience. But writing about such personal emotions in such a public forum also made her feel vulnerable. However, Lovato believed she was at the right place in her recovery to take this step. As the lyrics to the song go, "Now I'm a warrior. Now I've got thicker skin. I'm a warrior. I'm stronger than I've ever been."[c]

fee shop, a customer noticed a large cut on her arm and came right out and asked her if she had tried to commit suicide. This woman wrote, "Gotta love that SI [self-injury] has become 'mainstream' enough for people to joke about it, but not actually learn anything and take it seriously."[7]

While the public is more aware of self-harm today than it was a decade ago due to the media's coverage of celebrities who self-injure, there is still a lack of understanding of the issue and a strong stigma against people who self-harm.

If a stranger asks you about your scars, you may feel awkward and uncomfortable. Remember, you are under no pressure to reveal anything. Put your own needs first. The Cornell Research Program on Self-Injury and Recovery suggests that if someone inquires about your scars and you do not want to talk about it, you just simply say, "Thanks for asking but it's something I don't talk about with people I don't know well." Or you could say, "They are scars from a hard time in my life, but I'm not comfortable talking about it now."[8]

Educating the Medical Profession

Self-injurers, whether in recovery or not, can help raise awareness about self-injury disorder among front-line caregivers. Many school officials and medical professionals know little about this condition, and they are too often insensitive to the needs of people who self-harm. A self-injurer may seek treatment at an emergency room and encounter a nurse with little training in how to respond to SI. A teacher or coach might spot a recent scar on one of his students. A doctor might be the first person the self-injurer confides in when he comes in for an annual physical. Substantial evidence shows that few of these caregivers are adequately trained in identifying self-injuring. Nor do they know how to respond if they do suspect someone is a self-injurer.

A team of researchers from Finland conducted a literature review that analyzed 126 studies about self-injury. The results of their analysis were published in 2011 in the journal *Issues in Mental Health Nursing*. These researchers found that most nurses had trouble distinguishing between a suicidal patient and a patient who was a self-injurer. This could be because self-harm by teenagers is not studied in most nursing science programs where the focus is on adult, inpatient self-injurers. Therefore, nurses may treat a self-injuring youth as a suicide risk or an attention-seeking teenager, rather than someone with SI. School nurses, in particular, needed more theoretical knowledge and practical approaches for treating youth who self-injure.[9]

Self-injurers have a role to play in educating the medical profession. A 2010 documentary titled *A Silent Epidemic* features Nellie Worringham, a twenty-two-year-old Australian woman who has been battling self-harm since she was thirteen. Over the years superficial scratching gave way to deeper, harder cutting. Doctors told Nellie that she could kill herself one day if she does not stop. Nellie does not want to die, but sometimes it feels like the only way she can continue to live is by self-injuring. Despite serious injuries, Nellie has frequently been ignored or mistreated by medical staff when she sought emergency care. Because her wounds have been self-inflicted, but are not immediately life threatening, the medical staff often view her with disgust and treat her impatiently and callously. More than once Nellie has had to wait between four and six hours in an emergency room or clinic while people with much less severe injuries are treated.[10]

Even though she has not conquered her desire to self-harm, Nellie is fighting to improve the stigma she and other self-injurers face from the medical profession. She works with Professor Graham Martin at the University of Queensland in Australia to educate medical staff about self-harm. Nellie tells her story at medical seminars. She does not want other people struggling with self-injury to be disrespected and mistreated the way she has been.[11]

Nellie's is one just voice, but other voices are being raised as well. People around the world are trying to educate the public, advocate for improved treatment, and challenge the stigma against people with self-injury disorder.

College Student Activism

College is a time when you seriously begin to shape the future path your life will take. You learn exciting ideas, develop important skills, and meet a diverse mixture of people. Life on campus will mold you as you develop into a full-fledged adult. However, this impact can be reciprocal. Just as experiences on campus will shape you, so you too can impact the world around you.

When Alison Malmon was a freshman at the University of Pennsylvania, her brother committed suicide. He was a senior at the same school. He suffered from a mental illness but never shared this secret struggle. In response to her brother's death, Alison founded Active Minds in 2003. The goal of this organization is to combat the stigma of mental illness, including self-injury disorder. Many college students struggle with mental health issues, but are afraid or embarrassed to seek help. Active Minds seeks to end that stigma. There are now Active Minds chapters on more than four hundred college campuses. They link students with mental health resources in their communities and serve as the main voice for college students on issues related to mental health advocacy. Students involved in Active Minds chapters conduct annual educational campaigns such as the Stress Less Week and National Day without Stigma.[12]

Amanda is an example of a recovering self-injurer who decided to educate her peers about SI. Her involvement in Active Minds began as part of a project in a social work class she took during her junior year in college. Amanda was unsure how much she really wanted to be involved in this group. Although she had not self-injured for three years, she first harmed herself in the fifth grade and her shame about this past had deep roots. Then, in October of that year, she received a phone call. Her uncle had committed suicide. Amanda attended the funeral where she learned that some of her family had not been told the truth about how her uncle died. There was too much shame associated with the idea of suicide.[13]

This experience spurred Amanda to action. "I made the decision, then, to throw myself into Active Minds and fight the stigma associated with mental illness while linking people with support services before self-injury or suicide ever become an option."[14] She said that the opportunities for personal growth she has experienced working with Active Minds have been "immeasurable."[15] Active Minds is the organization that Amanda chose to become involved in. There are many others. Listen up during orientation. Look at the fliers posted in your student union or dorm lobby. Find a group in which you can use your talents to make a difference in the lives of young people who still struggle with self-injury disorder.

Movie Review: It's Kind of a Funny Story, *Directed by Anna Boden and Ryan Fleck, Focus Features, 2011*

You might think that suicide and self-injury cannot be funny, but in the 2010 movie *It's Kind of a Funny Story*, they are. Craig Gilner is under pressure. His father wants him to apply for a prestigious summer school program. Craig does not want to go but is afraid to tell his father. Increasingly desperate and depressed, Craig contemplates suicide. Afraid of his own emotions, he checks himself into an adult psychiatric ward. Craig soon realizes that his problems are nowhere near as severe as those of the people who surround him. These include the beautiful teenage Noelle, who self-injures, and Bobby, played by Zach Galifianakis. Bobby is a father who claims he is just on vacation, but later reveals that he has tried to kill himself several times. At one point Bobby reminds Craig to "just live."

And Craig does. The relationships he builds during his stay in the psych ward do not cure Craig's depression, but they do change him. He gets up the nerve to ask Noelle out on a date. He tells his dad that he does not want to apply to the summer school program, and he begins to pursue his passion for art. *It's Kind of a Funny Story* is funny because of the patients' fun-filled efforts to subvert the institution's rules. But on a deeper level, this is a movie about compassion and a story full of hope.

Grassroots Movements

Every year on March 1, look at the people around you. Some may be wearing orange clothes. A few may sport a purple and orange band around their wrists. Look a little closer. Can you read the letters printed on those wristbands? *New Thoughts, New Actions, SI Awareness.*

There are many awareness days. Some are silly and do not have a fixed date like Popcorn Day or Bubble Wrap Appreciation Day. Others are serious and widely known. World Aids Day is December 1, and Earth Day is celebrated on April 22. People around the world recognize March 1 as Self-Injury Awareness

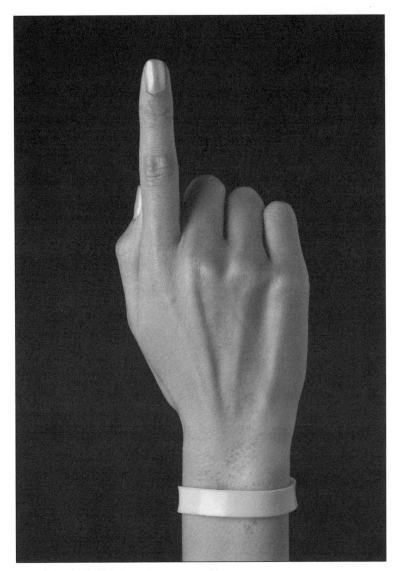

March 1st is Self-Injury Awareness Day.

Day (SIAD). SIAD has been recognized for more than a decade.[16] Not many people know about this day of awareness, but that is because SI is still a disorder that has only partially emerged from the shadows. SIAD is a small but growing movement to raise awareness of self-injury disorder and to educate people about the nature of this illness. Perhaps when March 1st rolls around, you will wear a purple and orange armband and let people know what it signifies.

We fear what we do not understand. The best way to combat stigma is through knowledge. So help the public understand what self-injury is and tell them how they can help the people who struggle with this disorder.

You might think, *I'm just one person. What can I do?*

A lot.

Write: Craft a letter to a local politician. Explain what self-injury is and ask your representative to advocate for research and treatment programs. Or compose a letter to the editor for your local paper. Describe what it is like to suffer from self-injury disorder.

Speak: Call your local radio and television stations and request that they do a news story on self-injury. Volunteer to be interviewed about your experience. If you are trying to reach an even wider audience than traditional media will capture, consider YouTube. That was the approach Jennifer took. She described the video she made on the website LifeSIGNS.

Although a lot of my friends and family were already aware of my history of self harm, I decided to make a YouTube video for Self-Injury Awareness Day this year, and share it with everyone on my Facebook. Initially I was nervous about how people would react, but I got very positive feedback from everybody, and was even called 'inspirational' by someone who watched the video! This made me feel much more positive about my experiences, like I'd been "forgiven" and that I have a body of supportive friends behind me if things get bad again![17]

Act: Organizations such as LifeSIGNS.org and Scar-Tissue.net have websites with downloadable fact sheets and posters. Print these. Distribute them in your school, your clinic, your workplace, your church.

Lead: Help your high school or college to develop a policy to identify and assist students who self-injure. Organize an event at your school on March 1st to spread the word about self-injury. One musician posted her approach on the website LifeSIGNS. She had taken a social action class in college. That experience spurred her to form an arts-based SI group on her campus. At the first meeting someone asked her why she had decided to organize this group. The musician had not intended to come out publically about her own history of SI, but the moment was right. So she said, "I used to SI for eight years and have been recovered for the past four. This is just something I'm really passionate about."[18] This woman does not feel the need to tell everyone she meets about her personal history. But she is not afraid to take action on this issue. She said, "Starting the social action group, raising money for SI treatment, blogging, and even joining the LifeSIGNS support forum. All of it combined makes me feel more open. And maybe one day it will be as easy telling someone as it is telling someone what the weather will be like tomorrow."[19]

Be creative: Social media is a great tool for raising awareness. Publicity stunts spread quickly. The Ice Bucket Challenge in the summer of 2014 resulted in people everywhere dumping buckets of ice water over their heads in an effort to raise money and awareness of Amyotrophic Lateral Sclerosis, the disease known as ALS. Between July 29 and August 21, 2014, the Ice Bucket Challenge raised almost 42 million dollars in donations to the ALS Association, a nonprofit group that funds research on treatments for this deadly disease. Celebrities from pop star Justin Bieber to former president George W. Bush joined the craze.[20]

Can you find a way to use your talent and passion as a tool to educate the public about SI? What ideas can you think of to educate people about self-injury disorder?

Be brave: If you have scars that you normally hide with clothing or makeup, choose one day a week to let your scars show. Recovering self-injurer and blogger Jennifer Aline Graham posted the idea of "Free Your Wrists Friday" on the blog *HealthyPlace.com*. She admitted that she has worn bracelets in public for the last ten years and feels very anxious when she forgets to put them on. She challenged her readers to exhibit their scars as a way to become comfortable in their skin and to prove to themselves how strong they are. Graham took her own challenge on August 9, 2014, and went to work without her bracelets. She felt uncomfortable and anxious all day and admitted to putting her bracelets back on when she left work. But she was proud of pushing the limits of her comfort zone. To deal with her anxiety she drank coffee and listened to a funny talk show. Graham said that "change is not comfortable, but sometimes it is needed."[21]

Read about It: Willow (New York: Penguin Books, 2009)

One rainy evening sixteen-year-old Willow Randall drove her mom and dad home from a party. They never made it. Willow lost control of the car and both of her parents died. Buried in pain and grief and guilt, Willow discovers that slashing her skin decreases an emotional pain so strong she is afraid it might kill her. But then Willow meets Guy, a boy in her new school. He soon discovers her secret coping mechanism.

The strength of the novel *Willow*, by Julie Hoban, lies in how the author reveals the complex nature of self-injury. Willow admits to Guy that she is not willing or ready to give up her razor blades. Cutting her skin is nowhere near as painful as the grief and guilt she feels about her parents. This novel is an honest portrayal of the process of recovery. People do not have an epiphany. They do not just flip a switch and stop their self-harm. *Willow* tells the story of the slow, halting, painful process of how a self-injurer heals.

Time for Change

What is your place in the self-injury struggle? Are you a parent desperate to help your child? Are you a teacher who wants to assist your student? Are you a friend who wants to help his buddy stop beating himself up?

Or are you a self-injurer?

Are you ready to reclaim your life?

This book has explored many aspects of self-injury from the history of this disorder to different treatments. Why and how this disorder manifests itself in certain people has been discussed. The recovery process has been examined. Different treatment options have been laid out. The voices of teens and young adults who have walked the hard path of self-injury have spoken.

Where are you in this story? The scars that mark your skin and your soul are part of your past, but new scars do not need to become your future.

A young woman named Taylor considers herself a warrior. She said, "I battled self harm. I cut myself for over a year. But I stopped recently. I still have my scars. I love them. They're my battle scars. They show that I won my fight."[22]

You will win your battle against self-injury too.

Notes

Introduction

1. Kate Kelland, "One in 12 Teenagers Self Harm, Study Finds," *Reuters*, last modified November 17, 2011, http://www.reuters.com/article/2011/11/17/us-self-harm-idUSTRE7AG 02520111117 (accessed January 31, 2014).
2. "Self-Injury, a Topic Not Often Talked About, May Affect 3 Million People." *Webster-Kirkwood Times Online*, last modified April 15, 2011, http://www.selfinjury.com/pdf/Webster %20Kirkwood%20Times.%20Self%20Injury%20A%20Topic%20Not%20Often%20 Talked%20About%20May%20Affect%203%20Million%20People%2015April2011.pdf (accessed January 31, 2014).

Chapter 1

1. Daniel Schorn, "Teen Shares Self-Injury Secret," *CBS News*, June 6, 2006, http://www.cbs news.com/news/teen-shares-self-injury-secret/. (accessed December 28, 2014).
2. Schorn, "Teen Shares Self-Injury Secret."
3. Schorn, "Teen Shares Self-Injury Secret."
4. Schorn, "Teen Shares Self-Injury Secret."
5. "Guys Self-Harm Too," http://kiwi-mate.tumblr.com/mystory (accessed November 22, 2014, but no longer available as of March 17, 2015).
6. "Guys Self-Harm Too."
7. Madalyn K. Hicks and Susan M. Hinck, "Concept Analysis of Self-Mutilation," *Journal of Advanced Nursing* 64 no. 4 (2008): 408–413, http://www.brown.uk.com/selfinjury/hicks.pdf (accessed January 3, 2015).
8. "I Self Harm," Experience Project, http://www.experienceproject.com/ (accessed March 16, 2014).
9. Susan Seligson, "Cutting: The Self-Injury Puzzle," *BU Today*, April 3, 2013, http://www.bu.edu/today/2013/cutting-the-self-injury-puzzle/ (accessed February 2, 2014).
10. Tracy Alderman, "Self-Injury: Does It Matter What It's Called?" *Psychology Today*, November 28, 2009, http://www.psychologytoday.com/blog/the-scarred-soul/200911/self-injury -does-it-matter-what-its-called (accessed February 2, 2014).
11. "Borderline Personality Disorder," National Institute of Mental Health, http://www.nimh .nih.gov/health/topics/borderline-personality-disorder/index.shtml (accessed February 5, 2014).
12. Patricia Adler and Peter Adler, *Tender Cut: Inside the Hidden World of Self-Injury* (New York: New York University Press, 2011), 1.
13. Adler and Adler, *Tender Cut*, 1.
14. Hicks and Hinck, "Concept Analysis of Self-Mutilation."

15. Adler and Adler, *Tender Cut*, 29.

16. Hicks and Hinck, "Concept Analysis of Self-Mutilation."

17. Kirstin Fawcett, "Myths and Facts about Self-Injury," *U.S. News and World Report*, December 26, 2014, http://health.usnews.com/health-news/health-wellness/articles/2014/12/26/myths-and-facts-about-self-injury (accessed December 27, 2014).

18. Patrick L. Kerr, Jennifer J. Muehlenkamp, and James M. Turner, "Nonsuicidal Self-Injury: A Review of Current Research for Family Medicine and Primary Care Physicians," *Journal of the American Board of Family Medicine*, October 12, 2009, http://www.jabfm.org/content/23/2/240.full (accessed February 2, 2014).

19. Jeffrey Kluger, "The Cruelest Cut," *Time* 165, no. 20 (May 16, 2005): 48–50.

20. Susan S. Lang, "Self-Injury Is Prevalent among College Students, but Few Seek Medical Help, Study by Cornell and Princeton Researchers Finds," *Cornell Chronicle*, June 5, 2006, http://www.news.cornell.edu/stories/2006/06/self-injury-prevalent-among-college-students-survey-shows (accessed February 2, 2014).

21. Lang, "Self-Injury Is Prevalent."

22. "I Self Harm," Experience Project.

23. Lang, "Self-Injury Is Prevalent."

24. "Ordinary Girl: Self-Harm," *Teen Ink*, http://www.teenink.com/hot_topics/what_matters/article/453904/Ordinary-Girl-Self-Harm/ (accessed December 29, 2014).

---

a. "Scars Tell a Story," *Teen Ink*, http://www.teenink.com/nonfiction/all/article/507747/Scars-Tell-a-Story/ (accessed February 7, 2014).

b. "Skin," *National Geographic*, http://science.nationalgeographic.com/science/health-and-human-body/human-body/skin-article/ (accessed February 2, 2014).

c. *Cut: Teens and Self-injury*, directed by Wendy Schneider, 2007, DVD.

d. "Songs about Self-Harm," Song Facts, http://www.songfacts.com/category-songs_about_self-harm.php (accessed December 28, 2014).

e. Cornell Research Project on Self-Injury and Recovery, home page, http://www.selfinjury.bctr.cornell.edu/ (accessed January 3, 2015).

f. Ronin Ro, "Garbage's Shirley Manson Admits to 'Cutting,'" *MTV.com*, May 30, 2000, http://www.mtv.com/news/1429321/garbages-shirley-manson-admits-to-cutting/ (accessed October 1, 2014).

g. Craig McClean, "Shirley Manson Interview: Breaking Up the Garbage Girl," *Guardian*, April 28, 2012, http://www.theguardian.com/music/2012/apr/29/shirley-manson-interview-garbage (accessed October 1, 2014).

Chapter 2

1. Herodotus, *The History of Herodotus*, trans. George Rawlinson, The Internet Classics Archives, http://classics.mit.edu/Herodotus/history.html (accessed November 27, 2014).

2. "The Flagellants Attempt to Repel the Black Death, 1349," EyeWitness to History.com, http://www.eyewitnesstohistory.com/flagellants.htm (accessed November 27, 2014).

3. V. J. Turner, *Secret Scars: Uncovering and Understanding the Addiction of Self-Injury* (Center City, MN: Hazelden, 2002), 114.

4. *The Holy Bible: New International Version* (Colorado Springs, CO: International Bible Society, 1984), Matthew 5:29 (p. 684.)

5. Turner, *Secret Scars*, 114.

6. Turner, *Secret Scars*, 30.

7. Marilee Strong, *A Bright Red Scream—Self-Mutilation and the Language of Pain* (New York: Viking, 1998), 32.

8. Strong, *A Bright Red Scream*, 32.

9. Strong, *A Bright Red Scream*, 32.

10. Armando Favazza, *Bodies under Siege: Self-Mutilation, Nonsuicidal Self-Injury, and Body Modification in Culture and Psychiatry* (Baltimore: Johns Hopkins University Press, 3rd ed. 2011), x.

11. Favazza, *Bodies under Siege*, ix–vi.

12. Favazza, *Bodies under Siege*, 4.

13. Favazza, *Bodies under Siege*, 10.

14. Favazza, *Bodies under Siege*, vi–xvii.

15. Patricia Adler and Peter Adler, *Tender Cut: Inside the Hidden World of Self-Injury* (New York: New York University Press, 2011), 18.

16. Jennifer Egan, "The Thin Red Line," *New York Times Magazine*, July 27, 1997, http://www.nytimes.com/1997/07/27/magazine/the-thin-red-line.html?pagewanted=9 (accessed November 24, 2014).

17. Egan, "The Thin Red Line."

18. Strong, *A Bright Red Scream*, 1.

19. Adler and Adler, *Tender Cut*, 167.

20. Adler and Adler, *Tender Cut*, 2.

21. Adler and Adler, *Tender Cut*, 1.

22. Kerry Grens, "Doctors Call Embedding a Severe Type of Self-Harm," *Reuters*, May 10, 2011, http://www.reuters.com/article/2011/05/10/us-embedding-idUSTRE74948P20110510 (accessed November 27, 2014).

23. Grens, "Doctors Call Embedding."

24. Grens, "Doctors Call Embedding."

25. Grens, "Doctors Call Embedding."

26. Bret S. Stetka and Christoph U. Correll, "A Guide to *DSM-5*," *Medscape Psychiatry*, May 21, 2013, http://www.medscape.com/viewarticle/803884_15 (accessed December 28, 2014).

a. "The Case of Helen Miller—Self-Mutilation—Tracheotomy," *American Journal of Insanity*, 34 (1878): 368–378, http://books.google.com/books?id=SEUXAQAAMAAJ&pg=PA368&lpg=PA368&dq=case+of+helen+miller+and+self+mutilation&source (accessed November 27, 2014).

b. "Karl Menninger, 96, Dies; Leader in U.S. Psychiatry," *New York Times*, July 19, 1990, http://www.nytimes.com/1990/07/19/obituaries/karl-menninger-96-dies-leader-in-us-psychiatry.html?src=pm&pagewanted=1 (accessed November 27, 2014).

c. Sylvia Plath, *The Bell Jar* (New York: Harper & Row, 1971), 117.

d. Plath, *The Bell Jar*, 148.

e. Sally Beddell Smith, *Diana in Search of Herself: Portrait of a Troubled Princess* (New York: Random House, 1999), 10–11.

f. "Diana's 1995 BBC Interview," *Frontline*, http://www.pbs.org/wgbh/pages/frontline/shows/royals/interviews/bbc.html (accessed November 27, 2014).

g. "Songs about Self-Harm," Song Facts, http://www.songfacts.com/category-songs_about_self-harm.php (accessed December 28, 2014).

h. S.A.F.E. Alternatives, home page, http://www.selfinjury.com (accessed January 1, 2015).

Chapter 3

1. James Owen, "Five Surprising Facts about Otzi the Iceman," *National Geographic*, October 16, 2013, http://news.nationalgeographic.com/news/2013/10/131016-otzi-ice-man -mummy-five-facts/ (accessed December 2, 2014).

2. "One in Five U.S. Adults Now Has a Tattoo," Harris Interactive, February 23, 2012, http://www.harrisinteractive.com/NewsRoom/HarrisPolls/tabid/447/mid/1508/articleId/970/ctl/ReadCustom%20Default/Default.aspx (accessed December 3, 2014).

3. "Body Modification and Body Image," The Body Project, Bradley University, 2014, http://www.bradley.edu/sites/bodyproject/disability/modification/ (accessed December 2, 2014).

4. "Minimally-Invasive, Facial Rejuvenation Procedures Fuel 5% Growth," American Society of Plastic Surgeons, February 19, 2013, http://www.plasticsurgery.org/news/past-press -releases/2013-archives/14-million-cosmetic-plastic-surgery-procedures-performed-in-2012 .htm (accessed December 3, 2014).

5. Larry Loh, "Thaipusam 2010: Faith, Ritual and Body Piercings," *CNN*, February 2, 2010, http://travel.cnn.com/singapore/play/highlights-thaipusam-2010-700793 (accessed December 2, 2014).

6. Jessica Firger, "Circumcision Rates Declining in U.S., Study Says," *CBS News*, April 2, 2014, http://www.cbsnews.com/news/circumcision-rates-declining-health-risks-rising-study-says/ (accessed December 3, 2014).

7. "Jewish Practices & Rituals: Circumcision—Brit Milah," Jewish Virtual Library, American-Israeli Cooperative Enterprise, 2008, http://www.jewishvirtuallibrary.org/jsource/Judaism/circumcision.html (accessed December 2, 2014).

8. Tracy Alderman, "Tattoos and Piercings: Self-Injury?" *Psychology Today*, December 10, 2009, http://www.psychologytoday.com/blog/the-scarred-/200912/tattoos-and-piercings -self-injury (accessed December 2, 2014).

9. K. Madalyn Hicks and Susan M. Hinck, "Concept Analysis of Self-Mutilation," *Journal of Advanced Nursing* 64, no. 4 (2008): 408–441.

10. Chole A. Hamza, Shannon L. Stewart, and Teena Willoughby, "Examining the Link between Nonsuicidal Self-Injury and Suicidal Behavior: A Review of the Literature and an Integrated Model," *Clinical Psychology Review* 32 (2012): 482–495.

11. Hamza, Stewart, and Willoughby, "Examining the Link."

12. Lori G. Plante, *Bleeding to Ease the Pain: Cuttings, Self-Injury, and the Adolescent Search for Self* (Westport, CT: Praeger, 2007), 2.

13. "Is Self-Injury a Suicidal Act?" Cornell Research Program on Self-injury and Recovery, Cornell University, http://www.selfinjury.bctr.cornell.edu/about-self-injury.html#tab6 (accessed December 3, 2014).

14. Hamza, Stewart, and Willoughby, "Examining the Link."

15. Plante, *Bleeding to Ease the Pain*, 9–10.

16. Hamza, Stewart, and Willoughby, "Examining the Link."

17. Hamza, Stewart, and Willoughby, "Examining the Link."

18. Hamza, Stewart, and Willoughby, "Examining the Link."

19. Hamza, Stewart, and Willoughby, "Examining the Link."

20. Hamza, Stewart, and Willoughby, "Examining the Link."

21. Patrick L. Kerr, Jennifer J. Muehlenkamp, and James M. Turner, "Nonsuicidal Self-Injury: A Review of Current Research for Family Medicine and Primary Care Physicians," *Journal of*

the American Board of Family Medicine 23, no. 2 (March–April 2010), 240–259. http://www
.jabfm.org/content/23/2/240.full (accessed December 6, 2014).

22. Hamza, Stewart, and Willoughby, "Examining the Link."
23. "Is Self-Injury a Suicidal Act?" Cornell Research Program.
24. "Conquering Self-Harm," *Teen Ink*, http://www.teenink.com/hot_topics/bullying/article/
    526344/Conquering-Self-Harm/ (accessed December 3, 2014).
25. Kerr, Muehlenkamp, and Turner, "Nonsuicidal Self-Injury."
26. Gratteciel, "When Was Your First Time Cutting," Psychforums.com, May 5, 2012, http://
    www.psychforums.com/cutting-self-injury/topic63594-50.html (accessed December 3,
    2014).
27. Kate Lunau, "Teenagers Wired to Take Risks," *Maclean's* 124, no. 13 (2011): 51, Academic
    Search Premier, EBSCOhost.
28. Armando Favazza, *Bodies under Siege: Self-Mutilation, Nonsuicidal Self-Injury, and Body
    Modification in Culture and Psychiatry*, 3rd ed. (Baltimore: Johns Hopkins University Press,
    2011), 209.
29. Favazza, *Bodies under Siege*, 209–210.
30. Favazza, *Bodies under Siege*, 211.
31. Favazza, *Bodies under Siege*, 212.
32. Favazza, *Bodies under Siege*, 139.
33. Favazza, *Bodies under Siege*, 140.
34. Barbara Natterson-Horowitz and Kathyrn Bowers, "Our Animal Natures," *New York Times*,
    Sunday Review, June 9, 2012, http://www.nytimes.com/2012/06/10/opinion/sunday/our
    -animal-natures.html?pagewanted=all&_r=0 (accessed December 6, 2014).
35. Favazza, *Bodies under Siege*, 212.
36. Favazza, *Bodies under Siege*, 213–215.
37. Amanda Purington and Janis Whitlock, "Self-Injury Fact Sheet," ACT for Youth Upstate
    Center of Excellence, 2004, http://www.selfinjury.com/pdf/ACT%20for%20Youth%20
    Upstate%20Center%20of%20Excellence.SI%20Fact%20Sheet.Aug04.pdf (accessed March
    12, 2015).
38. Kerr, Muehlenkamp, and Turner, "Nonsuicidal Self-Injury."
39. Karen Conterio and Wendy Lader, *Bodily Harm: The Breakthrough Treatment Program for
    Self-Injurers* (New York: Hyperion, 1998), 16–17.
40. Amanda Booker and Karene Purington, "Understanding Self-Injury," Department of
    Human Development, Cornell University, http://www.human.cornell.edu/hd/outreach
    -extension/upload/CHE_HD_Self_Injury-final.pdf (accessed December 7, 2014).
41. Natasha Tracy, "10 Ways People Self-Harm, Self-Injure," *HealthyPlace* (blog), July 4, 2013,
    http://www.healthyplace.com/abuse/self-injury/10-ways-people-self-harm-self-injure/ (ac-
    cessed December 6, 2014).
42. Tracy, "10 Ways People Self-Harm, Self-Injure."
43. Jeffrey Kluger, "The Cruelest CUT," *Time* 165, no. 20 (May 16, 2005): 48–50. Academic
    Search Premier, EBSCOhost.
44. Kris, "I'm a Cutter. A Teenager Cutting Myself," Healthy Place, July 5, 2013, http://www
    .healthyplace.com/abuse/self-injury/im-a-cutter-a-teenager-cutting-myself/ (accessed De-
    cember 6, 2014).
45. Tracy, "10 Ways People Self-Harm, Self-Injure."
46. Tracy, "10 Ways People Self-Harm, Self-Injure."
47. Adler and Adler, *Tender Cut*, 63.

48. Adler and Adler, *Tender Cut*, 63.

49. Adler and Adler, *Tender Cut*, 7.

50. Kerr, Muehlenkamp, and Turner. "Nonsuicidal Self-Injury."

51. Adler and Adler, *Tender Cut*, 64.

52. Conterio and Lader, *Bodily Harm*, 18.

53. Hicks and Hinck, "Concept Analysis of Self-Mutilation."

54. Self-Injury.net, http://self-injury.net/ (accessed October 10, 2014).

55. Adler and Adler, *Tender Cut*, 63.

a. Allison Adato, "Obsessed with Plastic Surgery," *People*, January 16, 2007, http://www.people.com/people/archive/article/0,,20062412,00.html (accessed December 3, 2014).

b. Nicole Frehsee, "Amy Winehouse: Biography," *Rolling Stone*, http://www.rollingstone.com/music/artists/amy-winehouse/biography (accessed December 31, 2014).

c. Jenny Eliscu, "Amy Winehouse: A Troubled Star Gone Too Soon," *Rolling Stone*, July 24, 201, http://www.rollingstone.com/music/news/amy-winehouses-death-a-troubled-star-gone-too-soon-20110724?page=2 (accessed December 31, 2014).

d. DesireeAmy, "That Cut Could Be the Death of Me," *Teen Ink*, August 8, 2014, http://www.teenink.com/opinion/social_issues_civics/article/560468/That-Cut-Could-Be-The-Death-Of-Me/ (accessed December 4, 2014).

e. "Songs about Self-Harm," Song Facts, http://www.songfacts.com/category-songs_about_self-harm.php (accessed December 28, 2014).

f. "Amanda Palmer," SongFacts, http://www.songfacts.com/blog/interviews/amanda_palmer/ (accessed March 12, 2015).

g. Christine Montross, "The Woman Who Ate Cutlery," *New York Times*, August 3, 2013, http://www.nytimes.com/2013/08/04/opinion/sunday/the-woman-who-ate-cutlery.html?emc=eta1&_r=0 (accessed December 4, 2014).

h. David Fitzpatrick, *Sharp: A Memoir* (New York: HarperCollins, 2012).

i. Poetic_chaos, "Sharp," *Teen Ink*, August 10, 2014, http://www.teenink.com/poetry/ballad/article/576019/Sharp/ (accessed December 3, 2014).

j. Adolescent Self-Injury Foundation, home page, http://www.adolescentselfinjuryfoundation.com/page1 (accessed December 3, 2014).

Chapter 4

1. Karen Conterio and Wendy Lader, *Bodily Harm: The Breakthrough Treatment Program for Self-Injurers* (New York: Hyperion, 1998), 19.

2. Jack Mazurak, "Self-Harm Study of Miss. Youth Finds Highest Rate in African-American Males," University of Mississippi Medical Center, http://www.umc.edu/news_and_publications/press_release/2012-05-14-00_self_harm_study_of_miss__youth_finds_highest_rate_in_african-american_males.aspx (accessed December 7, 2014).

3. Mazurak, "Self-Harm Study of Miss. Youth."

4. Mazurak, "Self-Harm Study of Miss. Youth."

5. Megan S. Chesin, Aviva N. Moster, and Elizabeth L. Jeglic, "Non-Suicidal Self-Injury among Ethnically and Racially Diverse Emerging Adults: Do Factors Unique to the Minority Experience Matter?" *Current Psychology* 32, no. 4 (2013): 318–328, Academic Search Premier, EBSCOhost.

6. Chesin, Moster, and Jeglic. "Non-Suicidal Self-Injury among Ethnically and Racially Diverse Emerging Adults."
7. Chesin, Moster, and Jeglic. "Non-Suicidal Self-Injury among Ethnically and Racially Diverse Emerging Adults."
8. Chesin, Moster, and Jeglic, "Non-Suicidal Self-Injury among Ethnically and Racially Diverse Emerging Adults."
9. Sarah J. Nickels et al., "Differences in Motivations of Cutting Behavior among Sexual Minority Youth," *Child & Adolescent Social Work Journal* 29, no. 1 (2012): 41–59, Academic Search Premier, EBSCOhost.
10. Nickels et al., "Differences in Motivations of Cutting Behavior among Sexual Minority Youth."
11. "Somewhere over the Rainbow," *Teen Ink*, http://www.teenink.com/hot_topics/pride_prejudice/article/325126/Somewhere-Over-the-Rainbow/ (accessed December 7, 2014).
12. "Somewhere over the Rainbow," *Teen Ink*.
13. "Somewhere over the Rainbow," *Teen Ink*.
14. Madalyn K. Hicks and Susan M. Hinck, "Concept Analysis of Self-Mutilation," *Journal of Advanced Nursing* 64, no. 4 (2008): 408–413.
15. Lori G. Plante, *Bleeding to Ease the Pain: Cuttings, Self-Injury, and the Adolescent Search for Self* (Westport, CT: Praeger, 2007), 16.
16. Janis Whitlock et al., "Nonsuicidal Self-Injury in a College Population: General Trends and Sex Differences," *Journal of American College Health* 59, no. 8 (2011): 691–698, Academic Search Premier, EBSCOhost.
17. Whitlock et al., "Nonsuicidal Self-Injury in a College Population."
18. Amanda Purington and Janis Whitlock, "Self-Injury Fact Sheet," ACT for Youth Upstate Center of Excellence, 2004, http://www.selfinjury.com/pdf/ACT%20for%20Youth%20Upstate%20Center%20of%20Excellence.SI%20Fact%20Sheet.Aug04.pdf (accessed March 12, 2015).
19. Whitlock et al., "Nonsuicidal Self-Injury in a College Population."
20. Patricia Adler and Peter Adler, *Tender Cut: Inside the Hidden World of Self-Injury.* (New York: New York University Press, 2011), 35.
21. Adler and Adler, *Tender Cut*, 35.
22. Adler and Adler, *Tender Cut*, 13.
23. Plante, *Bleeding to Ease the Pain*, 22–23.
24. "Is Self-Injury Contagious?" Cornell Research Program on Self-injury and Recovery, Cornell University, http://www.selfinjury.bctr.cornell.edu/about-self-injury.html#tab9 (accessed December 3, 2014).
25. Kaba Fatos et al., "Solitary Confinement and Risk of Self-Harm among Jail Inmates," *American Journal of Public Health* 104, no. 3 (2014): 442–447, http://www.ncbi.nlm.nih.gov/pmc/articles/PMC3953781/ (accessed January 3, 2015).
26. Conterio and Lader, *Bodily Harm*, 131.
27. Conterio and Lader, *Bodily Harm*, 131.
28. Craig Bryan and Annabelle Bryan, "Nonsuicidal Self-Injury among a Sample of United States Military Personnel and Veterans Enrolled in College Classes," *Journal of Clinical Psychology* 70, no. 9 (2014): 874–885, Academic Search Premier, EBSCOhost.
29. Bryan and Bryan, "Nonsuicidal Self-Injury among a Sample of United States Military Personnel."
30. Bryan and Bryan, "Nonsuicidal Self-Injury among a Sample of United States Military Personnel."

31. Marilee Strong, *A Bright Red Scream—Self-Mutilation and the Language of Pain* (New York: Viking, 1998), 64.

32. Colleen M. Lang, and Komal Sharma-Patel, "The Relation between Childhood Maltreatment and Self-Injury: A Review of the Literature on Conceptualization and Intervention," *Trauma, Violence, & Abuse*, no. 12 (2011): 23, http://www.selfinjury.bctr.cornell.edu/perch/resources/lang-patel-2007.pdf (accessed December 7, 2014).

33. Strong, *A Bright Red Scream*, 65.

34. Strong, *A Bright Red Scream*, 66.

35. Strong, *A Bright Red Scream*, 77.

36. Plante, *Bleeding to Ease the Pain*, 20.

37. Judy Gershon, "The Hidden Diagnosis," *USA Today Magazine* 135, no. 2744 (2007): 72–74, Academic Search Premier, EBSCOhost.

38. Hal Arkowitz and Scott O. Lilienfeld, "The Cutting Edge," *Scientific American Mind*, 24, no. 5 (2013): 70–71. Academic Search Premier, EBSCOhost.

39. Strong, *A Bright Red Scream*, 109.

40. Strong, *A Bright Red Scream*, 111.

41. Strong, *A Bright Red Scream*, 112.

42. Kim Carollo, "Double Whammy: Eating Disorders, Self-Injury Linked, According to Study," *ABC News*, October 8, 2010, http://abcnews.go.com/Health/MindMoodNews/study-finds-link-eating-disorders-injury/story?id=11825071 (accessed October 15, 2014).

43. Strong, *A Bright Red Scream*, 114–115.

44. Strong, *A Bright Red Scream*, 114–115.

45. Kim L. Gratz and Alexander L. Chapman, *Freedom from Self-Harm: Overcoming Self-Injury with Skills from DBT and Other Treatments* (Oakland, CA: New Harbinger, 2009), 41–43.

46. A. Pawlowski, "Generation Stress? How Anxiety Rules the Secret Life of Teens," *Today*, September 17, 2014, http://www.today.com/parents/i-was-really-stressed-out-anxiety-rules-secret-life-teens-1D80148616 (accessed December 8, 2014).

47. Conterio and Lader, *Bodily Harm*, 63.

48. Maya Angelou, *I Know Why the Caged Bird Sings* (New York: Bantam, 1969), 78–79.

49. Strong, *A Bright Red Scream*, 39–40.

50. "The First Time," *LifeSIGNS* (blog), October 22, 2013, http://blog.lifesigns.org.uk/2013/10/the-first-time/ (accessed September 10, 2014).

51. Gratz and Chapman. *Freedom from Self-Harm*, 41.

52. Whitlock, "What Is Self-Injury?"

53. Adler and Adler, *Tender Cut*, 135–136.

54. V. J. Turner, *Secret Scars: Uncovering and Understanding the Addiction of Self-Injury* (Center City, MN: Hazelden, 2002), 22–37.

55. Mary E. Williams, ed., *Self-Mutilation* (Detroit, MI: Gale Cengage Learning, 2009), 14.

56. Strong, *A Bright Red Scream*, 57–58.

a. Russell Brand, *My Booky Wook: A Memoir of Sex, Drugs, and Stand-Up* (New York: Harper Collins, 2009).

b. "Ordinary Girl: Self-Harm," *Teen Ink*, August 11, 2014, http://www.teenink.com/hot_topics/what_matters/article/453904/Ordinary-Girl-Self-Harm/ (accessed September 10, 2014).

c. "Silverchair's Daniel Johns on His Recovery from Depression, Anorexia," *MTV News*, June 14, 1999, http://www.mtv.com/news/1434065/silverchairs-daniel-johns-on-his-recovery-from-depression-anorexia/ (accessed December 30, 2014).

d. Katie H, "Anxiety," *Teen Ink*, August 11, 2014, http://www.teenink.com/poetry/free_verse/article/570980/Anxiety (accessed September 10, 2014).

e. Architechtofmyownprivatehell, "Innocent Smile of Mine," *Teen Ink*, http://www.teenink.com/poetry/free_verse/article/448089/Innocent-smile-of-mine—a-selfharm-poem/ (accessed September 10, 2014).

f. Laurie Halse Anderson, *Speak* (New York: Farrar, Straus and Giroux, 1999), 9.

Chapter 5

1. Caroline Kettlewell, *Skin Game: A Cutter's Memoir* (New York: St. Martin's Press, 1999), 3–13.

2. Marilee Strong, *A Bright Red Scream—Self-Mutilation and the Language of Pain* (New York: Viking, 1998), 36.

3. Patricia Adler and Peter Adler, *Tender Cut: Inside the Hidden World of Self-Injury* (New York: New York University Press, 2011), 55.

4. Adler and Adler, *Tender Cut*, 53.

5. Adler and Adler, *Tender Cut*, 54.

6. Adler and Adler, *Tender Cut*, 54.

7. Adler and Adler, *Tender Cut*, 55.

8. Adler and Adler, *Tender Cut*, 55.

9. Adler and Adler, *Tender Cut*, 56.

10. Adler and Adler, *Tender Cut*, 58.

11. Adler and Adler, *Tender Cut*, 59.

12. Adler and Adler, *Tender Cut*, 61.

13. Adler and Adler, *Tender Cut*, 61.

14. Karen Conterio and Wendy Lader, *Bodily Harm: The Breakthrough Treatment Program for Self-Injurers* (New York: Hyperion, 1998), 32.

15. Conterio and Lader, *Bodily Harm*, 33.

16. Conterio and Lader, *Bodily Harm*, 33.

17. Adler and Adler, *Tender Cut*, 63.

18. Edward Selby, "Emotional Cascades and Self-Injury: Investigating Instability of Rumination and Negative Emotion," *Journal of Clinical Psychology* 69, no. 12 (2013): 1213–1227.

19. V. J. Turner, *Secret Scars: Uncovering and Understanding the Addiction of Self-Injury* (Center City, MN: Hazelden, 2002), 16–17.

20. Lori G. Plante, *Bleeding to Ease the Pain: Cuttings, Self-Injury, and the Adolescent Search for Self* (Westport, CT: Praeger, 2007), 40.

21. Plante, *Bleeding to Ease the Pain*, 42.

22. Conterio and Lader, *Bodily Harm*, 159.

23. Adler and Adler, *Tender Cut*, 69.

24. Adler and Adler, *Tender Cut*, 70.

25. Adler and Adler, *Tender Cut*, 70.

26. Conterio and Lader, *Bodily Harm*, 64-65.

27. Turner, *Secret Scars*, 97.

28. Adler and Adler, *Tender Cut*, 77–78.

29. Strong, *A Bright Red Scream*, 58.

30. Adler and Adler, *Tender Cut*, 78–79.

31. Adler and Adler, *Tender Cut*, 79.

32. Adler and Adler, *Tender Cut*, 81–82.

33. Adler and Adler, *Tender Cut*, 83.

34. Adler and Adler, *Tender Cut*, 84.

35. Adler and Adler, *Tender Cut*, 84.

36. Strong, *A Bright Red Scream*, 70.

37. Adler and Adler, *Tender Cut*, 86.

38. Adler and Adler, *Tender Cut*, 86.

39. Catherine Glenn and E. David Klonsky, "The Role of Seeing Blood in Non-Suicidal Self-Injury," *Journal of Clinical Psychology* 66, no. 4 (2010): 466–473.

40. Strong, *A Bright Red Scream*, 57.

41. Glenn and Klonsky, "The Role of Seeing Blood in Non-Suicidal Self-Injury."

42. Glenn and Klonsky, "The Role of Seeing Blood in Non-Suicidal Self-Injury."

43. Adler and Adler, *Tender Cut*, 87.

44. Adler and Adler, *Tender Cut*, 87.

45. Adler and Adler, *Tender Cut*, 87–88.

46. Adler and Adler, *Tender Cut*, 88.

47. Adler and Adler, *Tender Cut*, 88.

48. Kim L. Gratz and Alexander L. Chapman, *Freedom from Self-Harm: Overcoming Self-Injury with Skills from DBT and Other Treatments* (Oakland, CA: New Harbinger, 2009), 47–48.

49. Adler and Adler, *Tender Cut*, 88.

50. "The Contrast of Crimson," *TeenInk* http://www.teenink.com/nonfiction/personal_experience/article/482516/The-Contrast-of-Crimson/.

51. Adler and Adler, *Tender Cut*, 89.

52. Adler and Adler, *Tender Cut*, 89–90.

53. Adler and Adler, *Tender Cut*, 89–90.

54. Adler and Adler, *Tender Cut*, 91.

a. "Songs about Self-Harm," Song Facts, http://www.songfacts.com/category-songs_about_self-harm.php (accessed December 28, 2014).

b. Mark Beaumont, "Frank Turner: 'I Got 100 Death Threats a Day,'" *Guardian*, April 13, 2014, http://www.theguardian.com/music/2013/apr/24/frank-turner-death-threats (accessed December 29, 2014).

c. "Songs about Self-Harm," Song Facts.

d. "Interview: Trent Reznor," *Uncut*, May 4, 2005, http://www.uncut.co.uk/nine-inch-nails/interview-trent-reznor-feature (accessed December 29, 2014).

e. Larisa Brown, "Dame Kelly Holmes: I Used to Cut Myself and Even Thought of Suicide Because the Pressure to Win Was So Great," *Daily Mail*, September 16, 2012, http://www.dailymail.co.uk/news/article-2204005/Double-gold-Olympic-medallist-Dame-Kelly-Holmes-reveals-long-battle-self-harming-admits-thought-taking-life.html (accessed August 15, 2014).

f. "Holmes Reveals Self-Harm Ordeal," *BBC*, May 29, 2005, http://news.bbc.co.uk/sport2/hi/athletics/4590655.stm (accessed August 15, 2014).

Chapter 6

1. Laura Transue and Janis Whitlock, "Self-Injury in the Media," Cornell Research Program on Self-Injurious Behavior in Adolescents and Young Adults, 2010, http://www.selfinjury.bctr.cornell.edu/documents/media.pdf (accessed July 17, 2014).

2. Kate Daine et al., "The Power of the Web: A Systematic Review of Studies of the Influence of the Internet on Self-Harm and Suicide in Young People," *PLoS ONE* 8, no. 10 (2013), e77555, doi:10.1371/journal.pone.0077555.

3. Janis Whitlock, Jane L. Powers, and John Eckenrode, "The Virtual Cutting Edge: The Internet and Adolescent Self-Injury," *Developmental Psychology* 42, no. 3 (2006): 407–417.

4. Patricia Adler and Peter Adler, *Tender Cut: Inside the Hidden World of Self-Injury* (New York: New York University Press, 2011), 110–111.

5. "How Many Websites Are There?" *Tech Made Easy*, January 14, 2014, http://www.tech madeeasy.co.uk/2014/01/18/many-websites-january-2014/ (accessed December 17, 2014).

6. Adler and Adler, *Tender Cut*, 111.

7. "Safe Haven," Self-Injury.net, September 4, 2014, https://gabrielle.self-injury.net/forum/34 -rant-vent/ (accessed December 31, 2014).

8. Adler and Adler, *Tender Cut*, 113.

9. Peter Adler and Patti Adler, "How Has the Internet Affected Self-Injury?" *Psychology Today*, December 13, 2011, http://www.psychologytoday.com/blog/the-deviance-society/201112/ how-has-the-internet-affected-self-injury (accessed December 17, 2014).

10. Adler and Adler, "How Has the Internet Affected Self-Injury?"

11. Adler and Adler, "How Has the Internet Affected Self-Injury?"

12. Adler and Adler, *Tender Cut*, 112-113.

13. Daine et al. "The Power of the Web."

14. Whitlock, Powers, and Eckenrode, "The Virtual Cutting Edge."

15. Daine et al., "The Power of the Web."

16. Adler and Adler, *Tender Cut*, 118.

17. Daine et al., "The Power of the Web."

18. Adler and Adler, *Tender Cut*, 144–145.

19. "Cutting and Self Harm," Virtual Teen (forum), July 4, 2014 (8:32 a.m.), http://www .virtualteen.org/forums/showthread.php?t=210980 (accessed September 6, 2014).

20. "Cutting and Self Harm," Virtual Teen.

21. Adler and Adler, *Tender Cut*, 116–117.

22. Adler and Adler, *Tender Cut*, 125–126.

23. Whitlock, Powers, and Eckenrode, "The Virtual Cutting Edge."

24. Daine et al., "The Power of the Web."

25. Daine et al., "The Power of the Web."

26. Lori G. Plante, *Bleeding to Ease the Pain: Cuttings, Self-Injury, and the Adolescent Search for Self* (Westport, CT: Praeger, 2007), 39–44.

27. Maureen Salamon, "Dark Side of Chat Rooms for Troubled Teens: Talk of Self-Harm Strong Link Observed between Online Forums and Suicide Risk, Study Says," *U.S. News and World Report*, http://health.usnews.com/health-news/news/articles/2013/10/31/dark-side-of-chat -rooms-for-troubled-teens-talk-of-self-harm (accessed December 31, 2014).

28. Salamon, "Dark Side of Chat Rooms for Troubled Teens."

29. Amanda Purington and Janis Whitlock, "Nonsuicidal Self-Injury in the Media," *Prevention Research* 17, no. 1 (February 2010), http://www.selfinjury.bctr.cornell.edu/perch/resources/ non-suicidal-self-injury-in-the-media.pdf (accessed December 19, 2014).

30. Stephen P. Lewis et al., "The Scope of Nonsuicidal Self-Injury on YouTube," *Pediatrics*, February 21, 2011, http://pediatrics.aappublications.org/content/early/2011/02/21/peds.2010- 2317.full.pdf+html (accessed December 19, 2014).

31. Lewis et al., "The Scope of Nonsuicidal Self-Injury on YouTube."

32. Transue and Whitlock, "Self Injury in the Media."

33. Mary E. Williams, ed., *Self-Mutilation* (Detroit, MI: Gale Cengage Learning, 2009), 36.

34. Williams, *Self-Mutilation*, 89.

35. Williams, *Self-Mutilation*, 60.

36. Williams, *Self-Mutilation*, 60.

37. Caitlin Dewey, "Self-Harm Blogs Pose Problems and Opportunities," *Washington Post. com*, September 9, 2013, http://www.washingtonpost.com/national/health-science/self-harm -blogs-pose-problems-and-opportunities/2013/09/09/6f0ce85e-067f-11e3-9259-e2aafe5a5f 84_story.html (accessed July 16, 2014).

38. Transue and Whitlock, "Self Injury in the Media."

39. Williams, *Self-Mutilation*, 37.

40. "Marilyn Manson Simulates Wrist-Slashing after Dedicating Song to Paris Jackson," *Huffington Post*, June 8, 2013, http://www.huffingtonpost.com/2013/06/08/marilyn-manson-paris -jackson_n_3408099.html (accessed August 1, 2014).

41. J. L. Whitlock, A. Purington, and M. Gershkovich, "Influence of the Media on Self-Injurious Behavior," in *Understanding Non-suicidal Self-Injury: Current Science and Practice*, edited by M. Nock (Washington, DC: American Psychological Association Press), 139–156, http:// www.selfinjury.bctr.cornell.edu/publications/05.pdf, (accessed December 31, 2014).

42. Whitlock, Purington, and Gershkovich, "Influence of the Media on Self-Injurious Behavior."

43. Dewey, "Self-Harm Blogs Pose Problems and Opportunities."

44. David Murphy, "Instagram Removing Content That Promotes Self-Harm," *PC Magazine* 1 (2012), Academic Search Premier, EBSCOhost.

45. Murphy, "Instagram Removing Content That Promotes Self-Harm."

46. Dewey, "Self-Harm Blogs Pose Problems and Opportunities."

47. Krystie Lee Yandoli, "Inside the Secret World of Teen Suicide Hashtags," *BuzzFeed*, September 7, 2014, http://www.buzzfeed.com/krystieyandoli/how-teens-are-using-social-media-to -talk-about-suicide (accessed December 19, 2014).

48. Yandoli, "Inside the Secret World."

49. Yandoli, "Inside the Secret World."

50. Murphy, "Instagram Removing Content That Promotes Self-Harm."

51. Yandoli, "Inside the Secret World."

52. Dewey, "Self-Harm Blogs Pose Problems and Opportunities."

53. Dewey, "Self-Harm Blogs Pose Problems and Opportunities."

54. "Who We Are," Crisis Text Line, March 2012, http://www.crisistextline.org/who-we-are/ (accessed December 31, 2014).

55. "Who We Are," Crisis Text Line.

---

a. "The Interview," Beyond the Turn Table, April 4, 2006, http://www.randybrandt.net/btt/ interviews.php?id=iKutless06 (accessed December 30, 2014).

b. Chiderah Monde, "Justin Bieber Fans Draw Shock, Outrage with Gruesome 'Cut4Bieber' Trending Topic," *Daily News*, January 8, 2013, http://www.nydailynews.com/entertainment/ gossip/cut4bieber-trending-topic-draws-shock-outrage-article-1.1235624#ixzz39CBNQqVT (accessed August 18, 2014).

c. Hans T. Stermudd, "Photographs of Self-Injury: Production and Reception in a Group of Self-Injurers," *Journal of Youth Studies* 15, no. 4 (June 2012): 421–436 (accessed December 31, 2014).

d. Chris Heath, "Fiona: The Caged Bird Sings," *Rolling Stone*, January 22, 1998, http://www .rollingstone.com/music/news/fiona-the-caged-bird-sings-19980122 (accessed March 12, 2015).

e. "TWLOHA: Then and Now," To Write Love on Her Arms, http://twloha.com/vision/beginning (accessed September 21, 2014).

Chapter 7

1. Marilee Strong, *A Bright Red Scream—Self-Mutilation and the Language of Pain* (New York: Viking, 1998), 22–23.

2. Strong, *A Bright Red Scream*, 23.

3. Karen Conterio and Wendy Lader, *Bodily Harm: The Breakthrough Treatment Program for Self-Injurers* (New York: Hyperion, 1998), 159.

4. Lori G. Plante, *Bleeding to Ease the Pain: Cuttings, Self-Injury, and the Adolescent Search for Self* (Westport, CT: Praeger, 2007), 61.

5. "Recovery," Cornell Research Program on Self-Injury and Recovery, 2013, http://www.self injury.bctr.cornell.edu/recovery.html (accessed December 31, 2014).

6. "Two Sides of Self-Harm," *Teen Ink*, http://www.teenink.com/hot_topics/health/article/ 604154/Two-Sides-of-Self-Harm/ (accessed December 31, 2014).

7. "Recovery," Cornell Research Program on Self-Injury and Recovery.

8. "Two Sides of Self-Harm," *Teen Ink*.

9. Patricia Adler and Peter Adler, *Tender Cut: Inside the Hidden World of Self-Injury* (New York: New York University Press, 2011), 191.

10. Adler and Adler, *Tender Cut*, 191.

11. Adler and Adler, *Tender Cut*, 191.

12. Adler and Adler, *Tender Cut*, 191.

13. Adler and Adler, *Tender Cut*, 192.

14. Adler and Adler, *Tender Cut*, 193.

15. Adler and Adler, *Tender Cut*, 193.

16. Caroline Kettlewell, *Skin Game: A Cutter's Memoir* (New York: St. Martin's Press, 1999), 176.

17. Steven Levenkron, *Cutting: Understanding and Overcoming Self-Mutilation* (New York: W. W. Norton, 2006), 155–156.

18. Strong, *A Bright Red Scream*, 158–159.

19. Steven Levenkron, *Cutting*, 79–80.

20. Steven Levenkron, *Cutting*, 79–80.

21. V. J. Turner, *Secret Scars: Uncovering and Understanding the Addiction of Self-Injury* (Center City, MN: Hazelden, 2002), 137.

22. Turner, *Secret Scars*, 142.

23. Armando Favazza, *Bodies under Siege: Self-Mutilation, Nonsuicidal Self-Injury, and Body Modification in Culture and Psychiatry*, 3rd ed. (Baltimore: Johns Hopkins University Press, 2011), 158.

24. Favazza, *Bodies under Siege*, 166–167.

25. Turner, *Secret Scars*, 144.

26. Strong, *A Bright Red Scream*, 172–173.

27. Levenkron, *Cutting*, 81.

28. Favazza, *Bodies under Siege*. 262–263.

29. Favazza, *Bodies under Siege*, 262–263.

30. Plante, *Bleeding to Ease the Pain*, 86.

31. Plante, *Bleeding to Ease the Pain*, 93–94.

32. Plante, *Bleeding to Ease the Pain*, 91–92.

33. Turner, *Secret Scars*, 157.

34. *The Silent Epidemic*, directed by Ili Bare, Beyond Productions, 2010, documentary.

35. *The Silent Epidemic*.

36. *The Silent Epidemic*.

37. Turner, *Secret Scars*, 142.

---

a. ClarinetPower, "Bracelets," *Teen Ink*, http://www.teenink.com/poetry/free_verse/article/476219/Bracelets/ (accessed December 31, 2014).

b. "The Good Life—Night and Day Lyrics," MetroLyrics, 2013. http://www.metrolyrics.com/night-and-day-lyrics-the-good-life.html (accessed December 31, 2014).

c. Lawrence E. Shapiro, *Stopping the Pain: A Workbook for Teens Who Cut and Self-Injure* (Oakland, CA: Instant Help Books, 2008).

d. Chris Heath, "Johnny Depp—Portrait of the Oddest as a Young Man," *Details*, Johnny Depp Interview Archive, May 1993, http://interview.johnnydepp-zone2.com/1993_05Details.html (accessed December 29, 2014).

e. Miranda Sweet and Janis Whitlock, "Therapy: What to Expect," Cornell Research Program on Self-injury and Recovery, http://www.selfinjury.bctr.cornell.edu/documents/therapy.pdf (accessed July 17, 2014).

f. "Topic: What Are Your Thoughts Now about Your Scars?" Forum: Life after Self-Harm, (forum), January 22, 2013 (5:43 p.m.), http://buslist.org/phpBB/search.php?st=0&sk=t&sd=d&sr=posts&keywords=scars&fid%5B%5D=16&start=40 (accessed August 12, 2014).

g. LifeSIGNS, home page, http://www.lifesigns.org.uk (accessed December 31, 2014).

Chapter 8

1. Lori G. Plante, *Bleeding to Ease the Pain: Cuttings, Self-Injury, and the Adolescent Search for Self* (Westport, CT: Praeger, 2007), 62.

2. Karen Conterio and Wendy Lader, *Bodily Harm: The Breakthrough Treatment Program for Self-Injurers* (New York: Hyperion, 1998), 10.

3. Marilee Strong, *A Bright Red Scream—Self-Mutilation and the Language of Pain* (New York: Viking, 1998), 23.

4. Plante, *Bleeding to Ease the Pain*, 82–83.

5. Plante, *Bleeding to Ease the Pain*, 56–57.

6. Jarett Liotta, "Does Science Show What 12 Steps Know?" *National Geographic*, August 9, 2013, http://news.nationalgeographic.com/news/2013/08/130809-addiction-twelve-steps-alcoholics-anonymous-science-neurotheology-psychotherapy-dopamine/ (accessed December 21, 2014).

7. Conterio and Lader, *Bodily Harm*, 164.

8. Conterio and Lader, *Bodily Harm*, 164.

Bibliography

Books

Adler, Patricia and Peter Adler. *Tender Cut: Inside the Hidden World of Self-Injury*. New York: New York University Press, 2011.

Anderson, Laurie Halse. *Speak*. New York: Farrar, Straus and Giroux, 1999.

Angelou, Maya. *I Know Why the Caged Bird Sings*. New York: Bantam, 1969.

Brand, Russell. *My Booky Wook: A Memoir of Sex, Drugs, and Stand-Up*. New York: HarperCollins, 2009.

Conterio, Karen and Wendy Lader. *Bodily Harm: The Breakthrough Treatment Program for Self-Injurers*. New York: Hyperion, 1998.

Favazza, Armando. *Bodies under Siege: Self-Mutilation, Nonsuicidal Self-Injury, and Body Modification in Culture and Psychiatry*. 3rd ed. Baltimore: Johns Hopkins University Press, 2011.

Fitzpatrick, David. *Sharp: A Memoir*. New York: HarperCollins, 2012.

Gratz, Kim L. and Alexander L. Chapman. *Freedom from Self-Harm: Overcoming Self-Injury with Skills from DBT and Other Treatments*. Oakland, CA: New Harbinger, 2009.

Hoban, Julie. *Willow*. New York: Penguin Books, 2009.

Hollander, Michael. *Helping Teens Who Cut: Understanding and Ending Self-Injury*. New York: Guilford Press, 2008.

The Holy Bible: New International Version. Colorado Springs, CO: International Bible Society, 1984.

Kettlewell, Caroline. *Skin Game: A Cutter's Memoir*. New York: St. Martin's Press, 1999.

Levenkron, Steven. *Cutting: Understanding and Overcoming Self-Mutilation*. New York: W.W. Norton, 1998.

Moskowitz, Hannah. *Break*. New York: Simon Pulse, 2009.

Oates, Joyce Carol. *Two or Three Things I Forgot to Tell You*. New York: Harper-Collins, 2014.

Plante, Lori G. *Bleeding to Ease the Pain: Cuttings, Self-Injury, and the Adolescent Search for Self*. Westport, CT: Praeger, 2007.

Plath, Sylvia. *The Bell Jar*. New York: Harper & Row, 1971.

Smith, Sally Bedell. *Diana in Search of Herself: Portrait of a Troubled Princess*. New York: Random House, 1999.

Strong, Marilee. *A Bright Red Scream—Self-Mutilation and the Language of Pain.* New York: Viking, 1998.

Turner, V. J. *Secret Scars: Uncovering and Understanding the Addiction of Self-Injury.* Center City, MN: Hazelden, 2002.

Williams, Mary E., ed. *Self-Mutilation.* Detroit, MI: Gale Cengage Learning, 2009.

Journal and Newspaper Articles

Adato, Allison. "Obsessed with Plastic Surgery." *People.* January 16, 2007. http://www.people.com/people/archive/article/0,,20062412,00.html.

Adler, Peter and Patti Adler. "How Has the Internet Affected Self-Injury?" *Psychology Today.* December 13, 2011. http://www.psychologytoday.com/blog/the-deviance-society/201112/how-has-the-internet-affected-self-injury.

Alderman, Tracy. "Self-Injury: Does It Matter What It's Called?" *Psychology Today.* November 28, 2009. http://www.psychologytoday.com/blog/the-scarred-soul/200911/self-injury-does-it-matter-what-its-called.

Alderman, Tracy. "Tattoos and Piercings: Self-Injury?" *Psychology Today.* December 10, 2009. http://www.psychologytoday.com/blog/the-scarred-soul/200912/tattoos-and-piercings-self-injury.

Architechtofmyownprivatehell. "Innocent Smile of Mine." *Teen Ink.* http://www.teenink.com/poetry/free_verse/article/448089/Innocent-smile-of-mine—a-selfharm-poem/.

Arkowitz, Hal and Scott O. Lilienfeld. "The Cutting Edge." *Scientific American Mind* 24, no. 5 (2013): 70–71. Academic Search Premier, EBSCOhost.

Ballesteros, D. and J. L. Whitlock. "Coping: Stress Management Strategies." Fact Sheet Series. Cornell Research Program on Self-Injury and Recovery. Cornell University, 2009. http://www.selfinjury.bctr.cornell.edu/perch/resources/coping-stress-management-english-1.pdf.

Barrocas, Andrea L., Benjamin L. Hankin, Jami F. Young, and John R. Z. Abela. "Rates of Nonsuicidal Self-Injury in Youth: Age, Sex, and Behavioral Methods in a Community Sample." *Pediatrics* 130, no. 1 (2012): 39–45. http://www.ncbi.nlm.nih.gov/pmc/articles/PMC3382916/.

Beaumont, Mark. "Frank Turner: 'I Got 100 Death Threats a Day.'" *Guardian.* April 13, 2014. http://www.theguardian.com/music/2013/apr/24/frank-turner-death-threats.

Bell, Pooma. "Tried and Tested: HeadSpace Mediation for Modern Living." *Huffington Post.* July 30, 2013. http://www.huffingtonpost.co.uk/2013/07/09/headspace-meditation-benefits_n_3567421.html.

"Body Modification and Body Image." Body Project, Bradley University. 2014. http://www.bradley.edu/sites/bodyproject/disability/modification/.

Booker, Amanda, and Karene Purington. "Understanding Self-Injury." Department of Human Development, Cornell University. http://www.human.cornell.edu/hd/outreach-extension/upload/CHE_HD_Self_Injury-final.pdf.

"Borderline Personality Disorder." National Institute of Mental Health. http://www.nimh.nih.gov/health/topics/borderline-personality-disorder/index.shtml.

Brown, Larisa. "Dame Kelly Holmes: I Used to Cut Myself and Even Thought of Suicide Because the Pressure to Win Was So Great." *Daily Mail.* September 16, 2012. http://www.dailymail.co.uk/news/article-2204005/Double-gold-Olympic-medallist-Dame-Kelly-Holmes-reveals-long-battle-self-harming-admits-thought-taking-life.html.

Bryan, Craig and Annabelle Bryan. "Nonsuicidal Self-Injury among a Sample of United States Military Personnel and Veterans Enrolled in College Classes." *Journal of Clinical Psychology* 70, no. 9 (2014): 874–885. Academic Search Premier, EBSCOhost.

Carollo, Kim. "Double Whammy: Eating Disorders, Self-Injury Linked, According to Study." *ABC News.* October 8, 2010. http://abcnews.go.com/Health/MindMoodNews/study-finds-link-eating-disorders-injury/story?id=11825071.

"The Case of Helen Miller—Self-Mutilation—Tracheotomy." *American Journal of Insanity* 34 (1878). http://books.google.com/books?id=SEUXAQAAMAAJ&pg=PA368&lpg=PA368&dq=case+of+helen+miller+and+self+mutilation&source.

Chesin, Megan S., Aviva N. Moster, and Elizabeth L. Jeglic. "Non-Suicidal Self-Injury among Ethnically and Racially Diverse Emerging Adults: Do Factors Unique to the Minority Experience Matter?" *Current Psychology* 32, no. 4 (2013): 318–328. Academic Search Premier, EBSCOhost.

ClarinetPower. "Bracelets." *Teen Ink.* http://www.teenink.com/poetry/free_verse/article/476219/Bracelets/.

"Conquering Self-Harm." *Teen Ink.* http://www.teenink.com/hot_topics/bullying/article/526344/Conquering-Self-Harm/.

"The Contrast of Crimson." *Teen Ink.* http://www.teenink.com/nonfiction/personal_experience/article/482516/The-Contrast-of-Crimson/.

"Cutting and Self Harm." Virtual Teen (forum). July 4, 2014 (8:32 a.m.). http://www.virtualteen.org/forums/showthread.php?t=210980.

Daine, Kate, Keith Hawton, Vinod Singaravelu, Anne Stewart, Sue Simkin, and Paul Montgomery. "The Power of the Web: A Systematic Review of Studies of the Influence of the Internet on Self-Harm and Suicide in Young People." *PLoS ONE* 8, no. 10 (2013). e77555. doi:10.1371/journal.pone.0077555.

"Demi Lovato Talks about Self Harm" (Interview). YouTube video. http://www .youtube.com/watch?v=4oxxI3YnYnM.

DesireeAmy. "That Cut Could Be the Death of Me." *Teen Ink.* http://www .teenink.com/opinion/social_issues_civics/article/560468/That-Cut-Could -Be-The-Death-Of-Me/.

Dewey, Caitlin. "Self-Harm Blogs Pose Problems and Opportunities." *Washing-tonPost.com.* September 9, 2013. http://www.washingtonpost.com/national/ health-science/self-harm-blogs-pose-problems-and-opportunities/2013/09/0 9/6f0ce85e-067f-11e3-9259-e2aafe5a5f84_story.html.

"Diana's 1995 BBC Interview." *Frontline.* http://www.pbs.org/wgbh/pages/front line/shows/royals/interviews/bbc.html.

Egan, Jennifer. "The Thin Red Line." *New York Times Magazine.* July 27, 1997. http://www.nytimes.com/1997/07/27/magazine/the-thin-red-line.html ?pagewanted=9.

Eliscu, Jenny. "Amy Winehouse: A Troubled Star Gone Too Soon." *Rolling Stone.* July 24, 2011. http://www.rollingstone.com/music/news/amy-winehouses -death-a-troubled-star-gone-too-soon-20110724?page=2.

Fatos, Kaba, et al. "Solitary Confinement and Risk of Self-Harm among Jail In-mates." *American Journal of Public Health* 104, no. 3 (2014): 442–447.

Fawcett, Kirstin. "Myths and Facts about Self-Injury." *U.S. News and World Report.* December 26, 2014. http://health.usnews.com/health-news/health -wellness/articles/2014/12/26/myths-and-facts-about-self-injury.

Firger, Jessica. "Circumcision Rates Declining in U.S., Study Says." *CBS News.* April 2, 2014. http://www.cbsnews.com/news/circumcision-rates-declining -health-risks-rising-study-says/.

"The Flagellants Attempt to Repel the Black Death, 1349." EyeWitness to His-tory.com. http://www.eyewitnesstohistory.com/flagellants.htm.

Frehsee, Nicole. "Amy Winehouse: Biography." *Rolling Stone.* http://www.rolling stone.com/music/artists/amy-winehouse/biography.

Gershon, Judy. "The Hidden Diagnosis." *USA Today Magazine* 135, no. 2744 (2007): 72–74. Academic Search Premier, EBSCOhost.

Glenn, Catherine R. and David E. Klonsky. "The Role of Seeing Blood in Non-Suicidal Self-Injury." *Journal of Clinical Psychology* 66, no. 4 (2010): 468–473.

"The Good Life—Night And Day Lyrics." MetroLyrics. CBS Interactive, 2013. http://www.metrolyrics.com/night-and-day-lyrics-the-good-life.html.

Gratteciel. "When Was Your First Time Cutting." PsychForums.com. May 5, 2012. http://www.psychforums.com/cutting-self-injury/topic63594-50.html.

Grens, Kerry. "Doctors Call Embedding a Severe Type of Self-Harm." *Reuters.* May 10, 2011. http://www.reuters.com/article/2011/05/10/us-embedding -idUSTRE74948P20110510.

Hamza, Chloe A., Shannon L. Stewart, and Teena Willoughby. "Examining the Link between Nonsuicidal Self-Injury and Suicidal Behavior: A Review of the Literature and an Integrated Model." *Clinical Psychology Review* 32 (2012): 482–495.

Heath, Chris. "Fiona: The Caged Bird Sings." *Rolling Stone*. January 28, 1998. http://www.rollingstone.com/music/news/fiona-the-caged-bird-sings-19980122.

Heath, Chris. "Johnny Depp—Portrait of the Oddest as a Young Man." *Details*. Johnny Depp Interview Archive, May 1993. http://interview.johnnydepp-zone2.com/1993_05Details.html.

Herodotus. *The History of Herodotus by Herodotus*. Translated by George Rawlinson. Internet Classics Archives, 440 BCE. http://classics.mit.edu/Herodotus/history.6.vi.html.

Hicks, Madalyn K. and Susan M. Hinck. "Concept Analysis of Self-Mutilation." *Journal of Advanced Nursing* 64, no. 4 (2008): 408–413. http://www.brown.uk.com/selfinjury/hicks.pdf.

"Holmes Reveals Self-Harm Ordeal." *BBC*. May 29, 2005. http://news.bbc.co.uk/sport2/hi/athletics/4590655.stm.

"How Many Websites Are There?" *Tech Made Easy*. January 14, 2014. http://www.techmadeeasy.co.uk/2014/01/18/many-websites-january-2014/.

"The Interview." Beyond the Turntable. April 4, 2006. http://www.randybrandt.net/btt/interviews.php?id=iKutless06.

"Interview: Trent Reznor." *Uncut*. May 4, 2005. http://www.uncut.co.uk/nine-inch-nails/interview-trent-reznor-feature.

"Is Self-Injury a Suicidal Act?" Cornell Research Program on Self-injury and Recovery. Cornell University. http://www.selfinjury.bctr.cornell.edu/about-self-injury.html#tab6.

"Is Self-Injury Contagious?" Cornell Research Program on Self-injury and Recovery. Cornell University. http://www.selfinjury.bctr.cornell.edu/about-self-injury.html#tab9.

"Jewish Practices & Rituals: Circumcision—Brit Milah." Jewish Virtual Library. American-Israeli Cooperative Enterprise. 2008. http://www.jewishvirtual library.org/jsource/Judaism/circumcision.html.

"Karl Menninger, 96, Dies; Leader in U.S. Psychiatry." *New York Times*, July 19, 1990. http://www.nytimes.com/1990/07/19/obituaries/karl-menninger-96-dies-leader-in-us-psychiatry.html?src=pm&pagewanted=1.

Katie H. "Anxiety." *Teen Ink*. August 11, 2014. http://www.teenink.com/poetry/free_verse/article/570980/Anxiety/.

Kelland, Kate. "One in 12 Teenagers Self Harm, Study Finds." *Reuters*. November 17, 2011. http://www.reuters.com/article/2011/11/17/us-self-harm-idUSTRE7AG02520111117.

Kerr, Patrick L., Jennifer J. Muehlenkamp, and James M. Turner. "Nonsuicidal Self-Injury: A Review of Current Research for Family Medicine and Primary Care Physicians." *Journal of the American Board of Family Medicine* 23, no. 2 (March–April 2010): 240–259. http://www.jabfm.org/content/23/2/240.full.

Kluger, Jeffrey. "The Cruelest Cut." *Time* 165, no. 20 (May 16, 2005): 48–50. Academic Search Premier, EBSCOhost.

Kris. "I'm a Cutter. A Teenager Cutting Myself." *HealthyPlace* (blog). July 5, 2013. http://www.healthyplace.com/abuse/self-injury/im-a-cutter-a-teenager-cutting-myself/.

Lang, Colleen M. and Komal Sharma-Patel. "The Relation between Childhood Maltreatment and Self-Injury: A Review of the Literature on Conceptualization and Intervention." *Trauma, Violence, & Abuse*, no. 12 (2011): 23. http://www.selfinjury.bctr.cornell.edu/perch/resources/lang-patel-2007.pdf.

Lang, Susan S. "Self-Injury Is Prevalent among College Students, but Few Seek Medical Help, Study by Cornell and Princeton Researchers Finds." *Cornell Chronicle*. June 5, 2006. http://www.news.cornell.edu/stories/2006/06/self-injury-prevalent-among-college-students-survey-shows.

Lewis, Stephen P., Nancy L. Heath, Jill M. St. Denis, and Rick Noble. "The Scope of Nonsuicidal Self-Injury on YouTube." *Pediatrics*. February 21, 2011. http://pediatrics.aappublications.org/content/early/2011/02/21/peds.2010-2317.full.pdf+html.

Liotta, Jarett. "Does Science Show What 12 Steps Know?" *National Geographic*. August 9, 2013. http://news.nationalgeographic.com/news/2013/08/130809-addiction-twelve-steps-alcoholics-anonymous-science-neurotheology-psychotherapy-dopamine/.

Loh, Larry. "Thaipusam 2010: Faith, Ritual and Body Piercings." *CNN*. February 2, 2010. http://travel.cnn.com/singapore/play/highlights-thaipusam-2010-700793.

Lunau, Kate. "Teenagers Wired to Take Risks." *Maclean's* 124, no. 13 (2011): 51. Academic Search Premier, EBSCOhost.

"Marilyn Manson Simulates Wrist-Slashing after Dedicating Song to Paris Jackson." *Huffington Post*. June 8, 2013. http://www.huffingtonpost.com/2013/06/08/marilyn-manson-paris-jackson_n_3408099.html.

Mazurak, Jack. "Self-Harm Study of Miss. Youth Finds Highest Rate in African-American Males." University of Mississippi Medical Center. http://www.umc.edu/news_and_publications/press_release/2012-05-14-00_self-harm_study_of_miss__youth_finds_highest_rate_in_african-american_males.aspx.

McClean, Craig. "Shirley Manson Interview: Breaking Up the Garbage Girl." *Guardian*. April 28, 2012. http://www.theguardian.com/music/2012/apr/29/shirley-manson-interview-garbage.

"Minimally Invasive, Facial Rejuvenation Procedures Fuel 5% Growth." American Society of Plastic Surgeons, February 19, 2013. http://www.plasticsurgery.org/news/past-press-releases/2013-archives/14-million-cosmetic-plastic-surgery-procedures-performed-in-2012.html.

Monde, Chiderah. "Justin Bieber Fans Draw Shock, Outrage with Gruesome 'Cut4Bieber' Trending Topic." *Daily News*. January 8, 2013. http://www.nydailynews.com/entertainment/gossip/cut4bieber-trending-topic-draws-shock-outrage-article-1.1235624#ixzz39CBNQqVT.

Montross, Christine. "The Woman Who Ate Cutlery." *New York Times*. August 3, 2013. http://www.nytimes.com/2013/08/04/opinion/sunday/the-woman-who-ate-cutlery.html?emc=eta1&_r=0.

Murphy, David. "Instagram Removing Content That Promotes Self-Harm." *PC Magazine* 1 (2012). Academic Search Premier, EBSCOhost.

Natterson-Horowitz, Barbara and Kathryn Bowers. "Our Animal Natures." *New York Times*. Sunday Review. June 9, 2012. http://www.nytimes.com/2012/06/10/opinion/sunday/our-animal-natures.html?pagewanted=all&_r=0.

Nickels, Sarah J., N. Eugene Walls, Julie Anne Laser, and Hope Wisneski. "Differences in Motivations of Cutting Behavior among Sexual Minority Youth." *Child & Adolescent Social Work Journal* 29, no. 1 (2012): 41–59. Academic Search Premier, EBSCOhost.

"One in Five U.S. Adults Now Has a Tattoo." Harris Interactive. February 23, 2012. http://www.harrisinteractive.com/NewsRoom/HarrisPolls/tabid/447/mid/1508/articleId/970/ctl/ReadCustom%20Default/Default.aspx.

"Ordinary Girl: Self-Harm." *Teen Ink*. August 11, 2014. http://www.teenink.com/hot_topics/what_matters/article/453904/Ordinary-Girl-Self-Harm/.

Owen, James. "Five Surprising Facts about Otzi the Iceman." *National Geographic*. October 16, 2013. http://news.nationalgeographic.com/news/2013/10/131016-otzi-ice-man-mummy-five-facts/.

Pawlowski A. "Generation Stress? How Anxiety Rules the Secret Life of Teens." *Today*. September 17, 2014. http://www.today.com/parents/i-was-really-stressed-out-anxiety-rules-secret-life-teens-1D80148616.

Poetic_chaos. "Sharp." *Teen Ink*. August 10, 2014. http://www.teenink.com/poetry/ballad/article/576019/Sharp/.

Purington, Amanda and Janis Whitlock. "Nonsuicidal Self-Injury in the Media." *Prevention Research* 17, no. 1 (February 2010). http://www.selfinjury.bctr.cornell.edu/perch/resources/non-suicidal-self-injury-in-the-media.pdf.

Purington, Amanda and Janis Whitlock. "Self-Injury Fact Sheet." ACT for Youth Upstate Center of Excellence. 2004. http://www.selfinjury.com/pdf/ACT%20for%20Youth%20Upstate%20Center%20of%20Excellence.SI%20Fact%20Sheet.Aug04.pdf.

Purington, Mandy and Janis Whitlock. "Family Policies: Safety Concerns and Contracts." Practical Matters Series. Cornell Research Program on Self-Injury and Recovery. Cornell University. 2013. http://www.selfinjury.bctr .cornell.edu/documents/pm_family_policies.pdf.

"Recovery." Cornell Research Program on Self-Injury and Recovery. Cornell University. 2013. http://www.selfinjury.bctr.cornell.edu/recovery.html.

Rissanen, Marja-Liisa, Jari Kylma, and Eila Laukkanen. "A Systematic Literature Review: Self-Mutilation among Adolescents as a Phenomenon and Help for It—What Knowledge Is Lacking?" *Issues in Mental Health Nursing* 32 (2011): 575–583.

Ro, Ronin. "Garbage's Shirley Manson Admits to 'Cutting.'" *MTV.com*. May 30, 2000. http://www.mtv.com/news/1429321/garbages-shirley-manson-admits -to-cutting/.

Rothenberg, Patricia and Janis Whitlock. "Finding Your Voice: Talking About Self-Injury." Fact Sheet Series. Cornell Research Program on Self-Injury and Recovery. Cornell University. 2013. http://www.selfinjury.bctr.cornell .edu/perch/resources/finding-your-voice-2.pdf.

Rothenberg, Patricia and Janis Whitlock. "Wounds Heal but Scars Remain: Responding When Someone Notices and Asks about Your Past Self-Injury." Fact Sheet Series. Cornell Research Program on Self-Injury and Recovery. Cornell University. 2013. http://selfinjury.bctr.cornell.edu/perch/resources/wounds -heal.pdf.

Rothman, Michael. "'Pretty Little Liars' Star Opens Up about Self-Harming Past." *ABC News*. January 7, 2014. http://abcnews.go.com/Entertainment/ pretty-liars-star-opens-harming-past/story?id=21447374.

Salamon, Maureen. "Dark Side of Chat Rooms for Troubled Teens: Talk of Self-Harm Strong Link Observed between Online Forums and Suicide Risk, Study Says." *U.S. News and World Report*. October 31, 2013. http://health.usnews .com/health-news/news/articles/2013/10/31/dark-side-of-chat-rooms-for -troubled-teens-talk-of-self-harm.

"Scars Noticed." Buslist.org (forum). May 30, 2014. http://buslist.org/phpBB/ viewtopic.php?f=1&t=195104.

"Scars Tell a Story." *Teen Ink*. http://www.teenink.com/nonfiction/all/article/ 507747/Scars-Tell-a-Story/.

Schorn, Daniel. "Teen Shares Self-Injury Secret." *CBS News*. June 6, 2006. http://www.cbsnews.com/news/teen-shares-self-injury-secret/.

Selby, Edward. "Emotional Cascades and Self-Injury: Investigating Instability of Rumination and Negative Emotion." *Journal of Clinical Psychology* 69, no. 12 (2013): 1213–1227.

"Self Injury, A Topic Not Often Talked About, May Affect 3 Million People." *Webster Kirkwood Times Online*. April 15, 2011. http://www.websterkirkwood

times.com/Articles-i-2011-04-15-174540.114137-Self-Injury-A-Topic-Not-Often-Talked-About-May-Affect-3-Million-People.html#axzz3UDGBqLfo.

Seligson, Susan. "Cutting: The Self-Injury Puzzle." *BU Today*. April 3, 2013. http://www.bu.edu/today/2013/cutting-the-self-injury-puzzle/.

Sharples, Tiffany. "Teens' Latest Self-Injury Fad: Self-Embedding." *Time*. December 11, 2008. http://content.time.com/time/health/article/0,8599,1865995,00.html.

"Skin." *National Geographic*. http://science.nationalgeographic.com/science/health-and-human-body/human-body/skin-article/.

"Somewhere over the Rainbow. *Teen Ink*. http://www.teenink.com/hot_topics/pride_prejudice/article/325126/Somewhere-Over-the-Rainbow/.

Steele, Emily. "'Ice Bucket Challenge' Donations for A.L.S. Research Top $41 Million." *New York Times*. August 21, 2014. http://www.nytimes.com/2014/08/22/business/media/ice-bucket-challenge-donations-for-als-top-41-million.html?_r=0.

Stermudd, Hans T. "Photographs of Self-Injury: Production and Reception in a Group of Self-Injurers." *Journal of Youth Studies* 15, no. 4 (June 2012): 421–436. http://dx.doi.org/10.1080/13676261.2012.663894.

Stetka, Bret S. and Christoph U. Correll. "A Guide to *DSM-5*." *Medscape Psychiatry*. May 21, 2013. http://www.medscape.com/viewarticle/803884_15.

Sweet, Miranda and Janis Whitlock. "Information for Parents: What You Need to Know about Self-Injury." Fact Sheet Series. Cornell Research Program on Self-Injury and Recovery. Cornell University. 2009. http://www.selfinjury.bctr.cornell.edu/perch/resources/info-for-parents-english.pdf.

Sweet, Miranda and Janis Whitlock. "Therapy: What to Expect." Cornell Research Program on Self-Injury and Recovery. 2010. http://www.selfinjury.bctr.cornell.edu/documents/therapy.pdf.

Tracy, Natasha. "10 Ways People Self-Harm, Self-Injure." *HealthyPlace* (blog). July 4, 2013. http://www.healthyplace.com/abuse/self-injury/10-ways-people-self-harm-self-injure/.

Transue, Laura and Janis Whitlock. "Self-Injury in the Media." Cornell Research Program on Self-Injurious Behavior in Adolescents and Young Adults. 2010. http://www.selfinjury.bctr.cornell.edu/documents/media.pdf.

"Two Sides of Self-Harm." *Teen Ink*. http://www.teenink.com/hot_topics/health/article/604154/Two-Sides-of-Self-Harm/.

Whitlock, Janis, Jennifer Muehlenkamp, Amanda Purington, John Eckenrode, Paul Barreira, Gina Baral Abrams, Kerry Knox, et al. 2011. "Nonsuicidal Self-injury in a College Population: General Trends and Sex Differences." *Journal of American College Health* 59, no. 8: 691–698. Academic Search Premier, EBSCOhost.

Whitlock, Janis, Jane L. Powers, and John Eckenrode. "The Virtual Cutting Edge: The Internet and Adolescent Self-Injury." *Developmental Psychology* 42, no. 3 (2006): 407–417.

Whitlock, Janis and Mandy Purington. "Dealing with Power Struggles." Practical Matters Series. Cornell Research Program on Self-Injury and Recovery. Cornell University. 2013. http://www.selfinjury.bctr.cornell.edu/documents/pm_dealing.pdf.

Whitlock, J. L., A. Purington, and M. Gershkovich. "Influence of the Media on Self-Injurious Behavior." In *Understanding Non-Suicidal Self-Injury: Current Science and Practice*, edited by M. Nock. Washington, DC: American Psychological Association Press. 2009, 139–156. http://www.selfinjury.bctr.cornell.edu/publications/05.pdf.

Yandoli, Krystie Lee. "Inside the Secret World of Teen Suicide Hashtags." *BuzzFeed*. September 7, 2014. http://www.buzzfeed.com/krystieyandoli/how-teens-are-using-social-media-to-talk-about-suicide.

Organizations/Websites

Active Minds. http://www.activeminds.org/about/our-story.

Adolescent Self-Injury Foundation. http://www.adolescentselfinjuryfoundation.com/page1.

The Cornell Research Program on Injury and Self-Recovery. http://www.selfinjury.bctr.cornell.edu/.

Crisis Text Line. http://www.crisistextline.org.

Experience Project. http://www.experienceproject.com/.

LifeSIGNS. http://www.lifesigns.org.uk/.

National Alliance on Mental Illness. www.nami.org/.

National Mental Health Association. http://www.mentalhealthamerica.net/.

S.A.F.E. Alternatives: Self-Abuse Finally Ends. http://www.selfinjury.com.

Self-Injury.net. http://self-injury.net/.

To Write Love on Her Arms. http://twloha.com.

Films

Black Swan. Directed by Darren Aronofsky. Fox Searchlight. 2010.

Cut: Teens and Self-injury. Directed by Wendy Schneider. 2007. DVD.

Girl Interrupted. Directed by James Mangold. Columbia Pictures. 1999.

It's Kind of a Funny Story. Directed by Anna Boden and Ryan Fleck. Focus Features. 2011.

Prozac Nation. Directed by Erik Skjoldbjærg. Miramax. 2003.

Short Term 12. Directed by Destin Daniel Cretton. Animal Kingdom Traction Media. 2013.

The Silent Epidemic. Directed by Ili Bare. Beyond Productions. 2010. Documentary.

Thirteen. Directed by Catherine Hardwicke. Fox Searchlight. 2003.

Winter Passing. Directed by Darrell Larson. Twentieth Century Fox. 2005.

Index

About the Author

Judy Dodge Cummings is a writer and high school teacher in south-central Wisconsin. She has been a teacher for twenty-six years and holds bachelor's degrees in psychology and broad-field social studies as well as a master of fine arts in creative writing for children and teenagers. She has written several nonfiction books for young people, including *Civil War*, *Exploring Polar Regions*, and *The American Revolution: Experience the Battle for Independence.*